IN THE 21ST CENTURY
AN ANTHOLOGY OF ESSAYS

ESSAYS BY
DAVID BRIN · MATT BAI · MELISSA FEBOS
JAY STRONGMAN · MIKE SIEGEL · MARC POLITE
AND MANY OTHERS

EDITED BY
LORI PERKINS

For more information contact:
Riverdale Avenue Books
5676 Riverdale Avenue
Riverdale, NY 10471
www.riverdaleavebooks.com

Design by www.formatting4U.com
Cover by Scott Carpenter
Digital ISBN: 978-1-62601-359-9
Print ISBN: 978-1-62601-360-5

First Edition April 4, 2017

Table of Contents

Introduction
By Lori Perkins

There are books that you read that mark you, and stay with you forever. *1984* was one of those books for me.

I read it was I was 12. I grew up in Washington Heights, a decidedly middle class New York City neighborhood, then-populated with the largest residency of Holocaust survivors in the world (I had seen the concentration camp numbers tattooed on my friends' parents' forearms), and immigrants who had left warm-weather dictatorships to bring their children up in a land that offered freedom from what they had escaped. And yet, even at 12, I knew that freedom was subjective and fragile, as Watergate unfolded around me, and scared the shit out of me.

War is Peace was the unstated slogan of the Vietnam War.

Freedom is Slavery we were told as we were fought for civil and women's rights.

Ignorance is Strength was interchangeable for me with Reganonics.

That was my youth.

I reread *1984* every year until I graduated from college, and became a journalist (I became a journalist because of Watergate). As life got more demanding, I read it every other year. Then I stopped.

I married, had a son. Sent him to the same high school where I had studied *1984* (and *Brave New World*, *Walden Two* and *Fahrenheit 451*) in my junior year. I gave *1984* and *Lord of the Flies* to my son when he was 12, and he came back from a summer at camp to tell me that they were now his favorite books, beating out Orson Scott Card's *Enders' Game*. I was a very proud momma.

My son was a junior in high school in 2008, years after the year 1984 had come and gone, post-9/11. *1984* is no longer taught in high school. It is not taught at all (unless it's an elective in an advanced high school English dystopian fiction class or a college course).

This became painfully apparent to me recently when I bought a new smartphone at my local Verizon store where an extremely pleasant and technologically bright young man was helping me to upgrade. He noticed that one of the questions on my profile asked, "What is your favorite book?" and thought I had typed in a mistake when I filled in "*1984*."

"Is that a real book?' he asked.

I proceeded to give him a synopsis, to which he replied that he had never heard of it, and that he thought he might read it. He typed in a note on his cell phone, but, like one of the authors in this anthology, I happen to be in possession of quite a few dog-eared paperbacks of the novel, so the next time I went by the store, I dropped off a copy for him.

It made me wonder if *1984* was still relevant today.

I had asked myself that same question a few months before when I was in London and was surprised, and thrilled, to see that *1984* was playing on the London stage. I wondered if it might actually be the musical that included those *1984* songs by David Bowie ("We Are the Dead" and "1984") from his *Diamond Dogs* album (Bowie tried to get permission from Orwell's widow to do a musical, and she turned him down saying it would be in "bad taste.")

But I was able to secure tickets to the production (which offered a number of seats at each performance for the clever price of £19.84). I thought it was an opportunity to see a time piece, a relic from another era. I was astounded at how it still resonated, and that was way before Donald Trump's election as the 45th President of the United States.

Flash forward to November 9th, when I wrote in my journal (I have kept a long-hand journal since I was 12), "I went to bed with visions of a Brave New World, and I woke up in 1984."

As soon as Kellyanne Conway uttered her now infamous line about "alternative facts," I knew that I had to put this anthology together.

And then, of course, the world seemed to agree with me as *1984* made its surprise return to the No. 1 spot on the Amazon bestseller list.

As the London production of *1984* makes its way to Broadway, *Town & Country*'s Caroline Hallemann asks, "If 'Hamilton' was the Musical of the Obama Presidency, Is '1984' the Broadway Hit of the Trump's?"

It certainly is time to reread that book, or read it for the first time if you always meant to do so, or read it to or with your kids.

Or join thousands of other Americans on April 4th, 2017 as they go to 180 (and counting) movie theaters throughout the country where a one-time screening of the 1984 version of "1984," is being shown though the organizational work of the UnitedStateofCinema.com.

Now to be fair, Donald Trump is not the first politician to scare us into *1984* analogies. I am sure there were plenty of them during the Nixon Administration. And I know Obama's record on privacy and Freedom of Information documents release was far from stellar. Just who is Big Brother and who is Emmanuel Goldstein is up to the interpretation of the reader, or maybe they're one and the same? All the more reason to reacquaint yourself with this powerful book.

There are 25 essays in this book and they span the spectrum from academic treatises to personal reminiscences to political rants and screeds, and even fiction and theater. I think this collection truly shows just how the themes, language and messages of *1984* were part of the zeitgeist of the second half of the 20th Century. Their relevance to this new century seems pretty obvious.

1984 is a classic that should never be retired, and should always be taught. Many people thought it was a book about the future of the past. The future is now.

Lori Perkins
April 4th, 2017

George Orwell and the Self-Preventing Prophecy

By David Brin, Ph.D.

I propose that one of the most powerful forms of science fiction is the self-preventing prophecy. The prophecy that is so vivid that it marshals hundreds of thousands, even millions of people to prevent it from coming true.

This article was originally published in *Through Stranger Eyes*, a collection of Brin's book reviews, introductions and essays on popular culture, which was released in the Western Hemisphere by Nimble Books and in the Eastern Hemisphere by Altair (Australia). Included are his infamous articles about Tolkien and *Star Wars,* sober reflections on Jared Diamond's *Collapse,* and Rebecca Solnit's *River of Shadows,* scientific ponderings on Feynman and Gott, appraisals of Brunner, Resnick, Zelazny, Verne, and Orwell... all the way to fun riffs on the Matrix and Buffy!

It was originally written for "Orwell & Our Future," 50-year anniversary conference, 11/12/99, University of Chicago Law School. Parts of this paper were edited and revised from a series of articles about "The Coming Millennium" for Netscape's October, 1999, *iPlanet* magazine.

What will the future be like?

The question is much on peoples' minds, and not only because we've entered a new century. One of our most deeply human qualities keeps us both fascinated and worried about tomorrow's dangers. We all try to project our thoughts into the future, using special portions of our brains called the prefrontal lobes to mentally probe the murky realm ahead. These tiny neural organs let us envision, fantasize, and explore possible consequences of our actions, noticing some errors and evading some mistakes.

Humans have possessed these mysterious nubs of gray matter—sometimes called the "lamps on our brows"—since before the Neolithic Era. What has changed recently is our effectiveness at using them. Today, a substantial fraction of the modern economy is devoted to predicting, forecasting, planning, investing, making bets, or just preparing for times to come. Which variety of seer we listen to can often be a matter of style. Some prefer horoscopes, while others like to hear consultants in Armani suits present a convincing "business case."

Each of us hopes to prepare for what's coming and possibly improve our fate in the years ahead. Indeed, this trait may be one of the most profound distinctions between humanity and other denizens of the planet, helping to explain our mastery over the world.

Yet, it is important to remember that a great many more things might happen than actually do. There are more plausibilities than likelihoods.

One of the most powerful novels of all time,

published 50 years ago, foresaw a dark future that never came to pass. That we escaped the destiny portrayed in George Orwell's *1984*, may be owed in part to the way his chilling tale affected millions, who then girded themselves to fight "Big Brother" to their last breath.

In other words, Orwell may have helped make his own scenario not come true.

Since then, many other "self-preventing prophecies" rocked the public's conscience or awareness, perhaps helping us deflect disaster. Rachel Carson foresaw a barren world if we ignored environmental abuse—a mistake we may have somewhat averted, partly thanks to warnings like *Silent Spring* and the movie *Soylent Green*. Who can doubt that films such as *Dr. Strangelove*, *On the Beach*, and *Fail-Safe* helped caution us against dangers of inadvertent nuclear war? *The China Syndrome*, *The Hot Zone* —and even *Das Kapital*— arguably fit in this genre of works whose credibility and worrisome vividness may help prevent their own scenarios from coming true.

Whether these literary or cinematic works actually made a difference or not can never be proven. That each of them substantially motivated large numbers of people to pay increased attention to specific possible failure modes cannot be denied.

As for Big Brother—Orwell showed us the pit awaiting any civilization that combines panic with technology and the dark, cynical tradition of tyranny. In so doing, he armed us against that horrible fate. In contrast to the sheep-like compliance displayed by subject peoples in *1984*, it seems that a 'rebel' image has taken charge of our shared imaginations. Every conceivable power center, from governments and corporations to criminal and techno-elites, has been repeatedly targeted by Hollywood's most relentless theme... suspicion of authority.

Can you cite even a single popular film of the last 40 years, in which the protagonist does not bond with the audience by performing some act of defiance toward authority in the first ten minutes?

These examples point to something bigger and more important than mere fiction. Our civilization's success depends at least as much on the mistakes we avoid as the successes that we plan. Sadly, no one compiles lists of these narrow escapes, which seem less interesting than each week's fashionable crisis. People can point to a few species saved from extinction... and our good fortune at avoiding nuclear war. That's about it for famous near-misses. But once you start listing them, it turns out we have had quite an impressive roll call of dodged bullets and lucky breaks.

Learning why and how ought to be a high priority.

History is a long and dreary litany of ruinous decisions made by rulers in all centuries and on all continents. No convoluted social theory is needed to explain this. A common thread weaves through most of these disasters; a flaw in human character—self-deception— eventually enticed even great leaders into taking fatal mis-steps, ignoring the warnings of others.

The problem is devastatingly simple, as the late physicist-author Richard Feynman put it. "The first principle is that you must not fool yourself—and you are the easiest person to fool."

Many authors have railed against the cruelty and oppression of despots. But George Orwell focused also on the essential stupidity of tyranny, by portraying how the ferocious yet delusional oligarchs of Oceania were grinding their nation into a state of brutalized poverty. Their tools had been updated, but their rationalizations were essentially the same ones prescribed by oppressors for ages. By keeping the masses ill-educated, by whipping up hatred of scapegoats and by quashing free speech, elites in nearly all cultures strove to eliminate criticism and preserve their short-term status... thus guaranteeing long-term disaster for the nations they led.

This tragic and ubiquitous defect may have been the biggest factor chaining us far below our potential as a species. That is, till we stumbled onto a solution.

Each of us may be too stubbornly self-involved to catch our own mistakes. But in an open society, we can often count on others to notice them for us. Though we all hate irksome criticism and accountability, they are tools that work. The four great secular institutions that fostered our unprecedented wealth and freedom—science, justice, democracy and markets—function best when all players get to see, hear, speak, know, argue, compete and create without fear. One result is that the "pie" we are all dividing up keeps getting larger.

In other words, elites actually do better—in terms of absolute wealth—when they cannot conspire to keep the relative differences of wealth too great. And yet, this ironic truth escaped notice by nearly all past aristocracies, obsessed as they were with staying as far above the riffraff as possible.

Orwell saw this pattern, perhaps more clearly than anyone, portraying it in the banal and witless justifications given by Oceania apparachniks.[1]

How have we done with his warning? Today, in the modern neo-west, even elites cannot escape being pilloried by spotlights and scrutiny. They may not like it, but it does them (and especially us) worlds of good. Moreover, this openness has helped prevent the worst misuses of technology that Orwell feared. Though video cameras are now smaller, cheaper and even more pervasive than he ever imagined, their arrival in numberless swarms has not had the totalitarian effect he prophesied, perhaps because—forewarned—we act to ensure that the lenses point both ways.

This knack of holding the mighty accountable, possibly our culture's most unique achievement, is owed largely to those who gazed at human history and saw the central paradox of power—what's good for the leader and what's good for the commonwealth only partly overlap, and can often skew at right angles. In throwing out some of the rigid old command structures—the kings, priests and demagogues who claimed to rule by inherent right—we seem to be gambling instead on an innovative combination: blending rambunctious individualism with mutual-accountability.

Those two traits may sound incompatible at first. But any sensible person knows that one cannot thrive without the other.

The Orwellian metaphor is pervasive. On disputative websites like *Slashdot*, every third posting seems to blare warnings about "Big Brother," as adversaries scream "this is just like *1984*!" whenever something vaguely bothersome turns up (e.g. wall-sized television screens, personality tests for high school students, government surveillance cameras).

Is government the chief enemy of freedom? That authority center does merit close scrutiny... which we've been applying lately with unprecedented ardor. Meanwhile other citizens worry about different power groups—aristocracies, corporations, criminal gangs, and technological elites. Can anyone justifiably claim exemption from accountability?

Orwell's metaphors have been expanded beyond his initial portrayal of a Stalinist nightmare-state, to include all worrisome accumulations of influence, authority or unreciprocal transparency. Elsewhere I discuss the role that righteous indignation plays in helping to create what may be the first true social immune system against calamity. All four of those great social innovations mentioned above, that fostered our unprecedented wealth and freedom (science, justice, democracy and free markets), are based on harnessing this network of suspicion through vigorous and competitive application of mutual accountability. It may not be nice, but it works far better than hierarchical authority.

These "accountability arenas" function well only when all players get fair access to information.

Technological advances like the Internet may help amplify this trend, or squelch it, depending on choices we make in the next few years. The implications of burgeoning information technology may be enormous. Soon the cognitive powers of human beings will expand immensely. Memory will be enhanced by vast, swift databases that you'll access almost at the speed of thought. Vision will explode in all directions as cameras grow ever-smaller, cheaper, more mobile and interconnected.

In such a world, it will be foolish ever to depend on the ignorance of others.

If they don't know your secrets now, there is always a good chance that someone will pierce your veils tomorrow, perhaps without you ever becoming aware of it. The best firewalls and encryptions may be bypassed by a gnat-camera in your ceiling or a whistle-blower in your front office. How can you ever be sure it has not already happened?

Criticism is the best antidote to error. Yet most humans, especially the mighty, try to avoid it. Leaders of past cultures crushed free speech and public access to information, a trend Orwell showed being enhanced by technology in a future when elites control all the cameras. In part thanks to Orwell's warning, ours may be the first civilization to systematically avoid this cycle, whose roots lie in human nature. We have learned that few people are mature enough to hold themselves accountable, but in an open society, adversaries eagerly pounce on each others' errors. To preserve our freedom, we must not try to limit the cameras—they are coming anyway and no law will ever prevent the elites from seeing. Instead, we must make sure all citizens share the boon—and burden—of sight. This is already the world we live in. One where the people look hard at the mighty, and look harder the mightier they are.

Orwell's dark future can't come true if confident

citizens have a habit of protecting themselves by seeing and knowing.

Some businessfolk, like Jack Stack (author of *The Great Game of Business*), see the writing on the wall. By using open-book management, they reduce costs, enhance employee morale, foster error-detection, eliminate layers of management, speed their reaction time, and learn how to do business in ways that make it irrelevant how much their competitors know.

Companies that instead pay millions trying to conceal knowledge will strive endlessly to plug leaks, yet gain no long-term advantage or peace of mind. Because the number of ways to leak will expand geometrically as both software and the real world grow more complex. Because information is not like money or any other commodity. It will soon be like air.

Let's take this a bit farther. Say you are walking down the street. Your glasses are also cameras. Each face you encounter is scanned and fed into an Internet pattern-recognition search.

Your glasses are also display screens. Captions accompany pedestrians and passing drivers, giving their names and compact bios. You do an eye-flick, commanding a fresh view from an overhead satellite. A tap of your teeth retrieves in-depth data about the person in front of you, including family photos and commentary posted by friends, business associates... even enemies.

As you stroll along, you know that others see you similarly captioned, indexed, biographed.

Sound horrific? Well, then here's the key question—how are you going to stop it? Outlawing the tools will only ensure that common folk can't use them. As Robert Heinlein said, the chief thing accomplished by privacy laws is to make the bugs smaller.

That, in turn, will only serve the interests of the mighty. As George Orwell would surely point out, elites (government, corporate, criminal and so on...) will get these new powers of sight, no matter what the rules say. So we might as well have them too.

The metaphor of Oceania's telescreen is central here. In Orwell's world, those at the top of a rigid pyramidal hierarchy controlled the flow of information with fierce totality. Only propaganda filtered downward, while every iota or datum about the lives of proles flowed upward. Accountability went in just one direction.

Despite repeated efforts by our own hierarchs to justify one-way information flows, the true record of the last generation has been an indisputable and overwhelming dispersal of knowledge and the power to see. People are becoming addicted to knowing. Take the events that surrounded the tragedies of September 11, 2001. Most of the video we saw was taken by private citizens, a potentially crucial element in future emergencies. Private cell phones spread word quicker than official media. So did email and instant messaging when the telephone system got swamped. Swarms of volunteers descended on the disaster sites, as local officials quickly dropped their everyday concerns about liability or professional status in order to use all willing hands. The sole effective action to thwart terrorist plans was taken by individuals aboard United Flight 93, armed with intelligence and communication tools—and a mandate—outside official channels.

Is this a true and unstoppable trend? I speak of this elsewhere. Has it been, in part driven by the inoculative effects of cautionary fiction such as *1984*? I can't even begin to prove the hypothesis. Is this a different way to look at the effects and importance of literature? You bet it is. Scholars aren't used to considering the pragmatic fruits of fictional gedankenexperimentation, but perhaps it's time they started.

Consider the issue of these dispersed information systems from another perspective. The best analogy I can come up with is the old villages that our ancestors lived in, till just a few decades ago. They, too, knew intimate details about almost everyone they met on a given day. Back then, you recognized maybe a thousand people. But we won't be limited by the capacity of organic vision and memory. Our enhanced eyes will scan ten billion fellow villagers. Our enhanced memories will know their reputations, and they will know ours.

This is obviously cause for mixed feelings and deep misgivings. Will it be the egalitarian "good village" of Andy Hardy movies... safe, egalitarian and warmly tolerant of eccentricity? Or the bad village of Frank Capra's *Potterstown*, a place steeped in hierarchies, feuds and petty bigotries, where the mighty and the narrow-minded suppress all deviance from dismal normality?

Or even the vast, stifling, all-knowing 'village' of Orwell's Oceania?

We'd better start arguing about this now—how to make the scary parts less scary, and the good parts better—because the village is coming back, like it or not.

The key to our success—both personal and as a society—will be agility in dealing with whatever the future hurls our way. Moreover, there are reasons to think we already have what it takes. Consider the following hoary old cliché.

"Too bad human decency and justice haven't kept pace with our technological progress."

Here is another.

"No past era featured as much cruelty and misery as this one."

People seem to draw perverse pleasure from such statements, even though they are patently false.

In fact, over half of those alive on Earth today have never seen war, starvation or major civil strife with their own eyes. Most never went more than a day without food. Only a small fraction have seen a city burn, heard the footsteps of a conquering army, or watched an overlord exercise capricious power of life and death over helpless serfs. Yet these events were routine for most of our ancestors.

Of course, when I speak of fractions that still leaves hundreds of millions who have experienced such things! I won't minimize the terrors so many still endure. Our consciences should be prodded by the relentless power of television, into compassion and vigorous action.

Still, it's worth noting that things have changed a bit since humanity wallowed in horror, back in the middle years of the 20th Century. The ratio of humans who now live modestly safe and comfortable lives— (though in conditions modern North Americans might deem scanty)—has never been greater. It means the slope hasn't been all down, since the despair of 1942. Some might even argue that progress has been made.

As for comparing technical and moral advances, there's just no contest. For example, while I truly love the Internet, its effects on real life have so far been rather exaggerated. Telephones and radio had far greater immediate effects on people's lives when they entered the home, opening the world to millions.

It is our attitudes—toward all sorts of injustices that used to be considered inherent—that have undergone a transformation unlike any in history.

Consider the famous Stanley Kubrick film, *2001: A Space Odyssey.* Way back when it appeared, in 1967, two monumental projects transfixed the people of the United States—conquering outer space and tackling injustice to achieve a more honorable society.

Who would have imagined, back then, that colonizing space would prove such a grindingly slow job... yet by 1999 we would take for granted so many advances in tolerance, decency and accountability? Or that we'd so ignore these achievements, focusing instead on the residual injustices that are left unsolved?

We still don't have the fancy space stations of *2001...* but there is another, more important difference. Our astronauts today come in all sexes and colors. Any kids who watch them on TV feel a bit less fettered by presumed limitations. Each of them may choose to hope, or not, without being told you can't.

At this rate, who will bet me that a woman won't preside in the White House long before the first human being steps on Mars? Progress doesn't always go the way you expect it to.

This is not the path prophesied in *1984*, which envisioned a bitter society—one that exploited every opportunity to stoke hatred and division among the ruled. One in which the common man is little better than a harried sheep, ignorant, disempowered and unable to imagine another way. So far, we seem aimed at avoiding that particular failure mode. (At least those who read science fiction cannot be accused of lacking imagination.)

Do we owe this fact, in part, to anti-Cassandras like George Orwell whose warnings, once they were heeded, thus never came true?

Is fear of dystopian nightmare a greater motivator and effectuator of change than any utopian promise? Indeed, our tendency seems always to criticize whatever injustices remain unsolved, rather than ever pause to rejoice in what's been accomplished. That alone shows how deeply the lesson has been learned.

The worry that Orwell and others ignited in us still burns. It drives us on, far more effectively than any vague glowing promise of a better world.

We daren't let up. Not ever, because we've been shown the alternatives.

The world that George Orwell presented was—and remains—just too scary.

---

[1]Orwell's books are often cited as warnings against science and technology... a terrible misinterpretation. While Oceania's tyrants gladly use certain technological tools to reinforce their grip on power, their order stifles every human ingredient needed for science and free enquiry. Beyond tools of suppression and surveillance, technology is stagnant, productivity

declining. Innovation is subversive. It is a society that eats its seed corn and beats plowshares into useless statues. Yet, many critics persuade themselves that the Oceania elite, while evil, is somehow clever at the same time.

A similar fixation can be seen in popular interpretations of Mary Shelley's masterwork, *Frankenstein*, which is widely perceived as a polemic against science and the arrogation of God's powers. Yet, Shelley herself does not seem to hold that view. The 'creature' begins in innocence and a state of tentative hopefulness. It is Victor Frankenstein's subsequent behavior that earns the reader's contempt. Frankenstein's vicious rejection and cruelty toward his own creation is the fault that brings pain to his world and unleashes his great punishment. Rather than rejecting science, the novel's moral appears to be "don't be a lousy dad." (Which is interesting, given Mary Shelley's personal background.)

The central lesson of both tales is that technology can be abused when it is monopolized by a narrow, secretive and self-deceiving elite, absent any accountability or outside criticism. Almost any modern scientist would call this obvious. And after growing up with such stories, many non-scientists find it apparent, as well. The warning is heard.

David Brin is a scientist and best-selling author whose future-oriented novels include *Earth, The Postman*, and Hugo Award winners *Startide Rising* and *The Uplift War.* (***The Postman*** inspired a major film in 1998.) Brin is also known as a leading commentator on modern technological trends. His nonfiction book—*The Transparent Society*—won the Freedom of Speech Award of the American Library Association. Brin's newest novel *Existence* explores the ultimate question: Billions of planets may be ripe for life, even intelligence. So where is Everybody?

Although he explores many fields, heedless of credentials, Brin does have degrees from Caltech and UCSD (PhD in Physics, working with Nobelist Hannes Alfven). As a speaker Brin shares unique and often-humorous insights to the way technology may affect our human future.

1984 Was the Catalyst of Our Conversation
By David Jester

I was 25 and re-reading *1984*. The copy was a worn veteran of the used book business, purchased out of some 50 cent bin at one of those grocery stores along the back woods of Maine, where the ceilings seem dingy and dirty in the way a store that sells food shouldn't. Corners of the soft cover were missing. The upper binding had been chewed by some animal; I imagined a ferret, odiferous in nature, sinking its needle teeth into this classic. Part of the allure of an old, cheap book is analyzing the abuse it has received, imagining all the love that went into the wear that gave its patina. Each page was crisp and browned under my fingertips, paper that would soon crack at the turn of a page. In my possession, the book had traveled from Maine to Connecticut, and we were now adrift on a briny sea.

Crossing the Long Island Sound between Orient Point and New London is far from treacherous. I'd spent a significant portion of my life traveling to and fro on these boats, having lived on Long Island my first 18 years. Sitting on top deck, I sniffed the air, smelling the combination of diesel soot spewed from the smokestacks that rumbled next to me and the salt spray mixing with the wind splashed up and over the railings. I held my fingers tight to keep the pages from fluttering, and my cold hands reddened against the gales.

Engrossed in the words of Orwell, the world faded away, dissolving into that grey dystopian future of England… until a youthful voice shook me out of my imagination. "That book changed my life."

Who was he? I'll never know. I forgot to ask his name, so he will remain a spectre who floated in and out of my life in a brief moment. Around my age, he had wind burnt cheeks and short, strawberry blonde hair that moved with the wind like golden sea grass along the creeks feeding saltwater marshes.

He spoke confidently about *1984* without hesitation, as if I had telepathically asked for his opinion on the subject. The novel's thought-provoking message spilled from him with such zeal, and I absorbed his words and drank them with enormous thirst. He spoke of true freedom. We philosophized about citizens and the geographical boundaries of nations' borders, cultural constructs, society and the eventual breakdown of, and thought, pure thought. That book was the secret handshake. The I.D. into the club. The Masonic ring in literary prose. He wasn't just a believer of this Orwellian dystopian future, but an apostle of his ideologies.

I'd never connected with someone who felt strongly about *1984* before. As part of the required reading curriculum, I'd read *1984* the first time in high school, and I consumed it with an excitement bordering on fanaticism. I wasn't oppressed like

Winston Smith, but I was able to relate. My food wasn't rationed nor was I monitored by Big Brother through telescreens, but for me the world was always shaded in a grey tone. This book fed my rebellious, revolutionary and contrary personality. What I rebelled against was the inequalities and social injustices of life, and they surrounded me like an itchy wool blanket that irritated my skin with every movement of the day. My first rebellion was revealed before I was ever aware of such thoughts, with my forcible non-consenting baptism, so I remonstrated against what was ever present in my life, Catholicism.

In Catholic school, I was spoonfed catechism, forced to obey the teachings of the church, told to believe in God or face the penalty of eternal damnation. An oppressive force fought to dictate my thoughts and beliefs, as if my own convictions which did not align with the Vatican, somehow made me pariah, made me enemy of the state. Big Brother watched over me with dark eyes shaded within the recesses of habits, shadow figures channeling the word of God through their human form, armed with wooden rulers by their side.

I was a rebel simply because I questioned. Chided for my disbelief, my curiosity, I was told to get in line, to obey. My questions went unanswered by pious nuns and lay teachers who vehemently defended an antiquated system. All queries could be answered with one simple singular catchall: faith, Blind devotion did not settle well with me, and daily prayers reminded me of telescreens forcing a mantra, using mindless repetition to make me submit. Distinctive self-thought was tolerated and encouraged—as long as it did not go against ecclesiastical teachings. I, the eventual atheist, found myself amongst a group that wanted thought control, rather than thoughtful dialog and conversation.

Winston Smith understood; he commiserated in my struggle.

Orwell and *1984* were there to support me, to show me I was not alone.

And that day on the ferry, I realized I wasn't alone in how *1984* had resonated in my life. When the man on the ferry said,

"That book changed by life," he meant it. A self-appointed prophet, he believed the doctrine as set forth by Orwell with such zealotry that he took it upon himself to spread the word, or at least the book that contained the word. Finding cheap copies of *1984* in book bins, recycling centers, thrift and bookstores, this young man would purchase these books and then distribute them, leaving them in public spaces, with a note inside the cover, "Please read this book, it may change your life." He did not just read it, and walk away, having taken something from Orwell's message—he lived it. He contributed.

1984 inspires. It is not propaganda. It is not overt like the bible. The pages in this novel are not *Mein Kampf* utilizing fear of current events, xenophobia and racism to spur a movement through manipulative lies. *1984* doesn't take the worst of society and display it around every corner you turn. No, instead it shows an alternate view, the individual thinker amongst homogeneity, the self-aware amongst automatons, the unique where special is illicit.

Question. Think. Analyze. Don't just assume everything is OK, that the world is all right. Question why and at what cost it is the way it is. If anything, Orwell's opus was my first real instruction on critical thinking.

When I recently opened up my worn and weather-beaten copy of *1984*, that same one that elicited conversation on that ferry, the first page I opened up to had these words, separated on the page, as if calling to me, showing me how close we are to Orwell's vision:

"War is Peace. Freedom is Slavery. Ignorance is Strength."

In our country, in 2017, we've never been so close to this truth. With "alternate facts" emboldening the ideals of the willful ignorant, it validates arguments without truth, it strengths rhetoric which creates hate. The individual truth gets steamrolled by convenient soundbites. When our current leader calls the true enemy of our nation the free press he reads like the Inner Party, controlling thought, creating Newspeak, and making free thought and individualism a thought crime.

Dictators, authoritarians, totalitarians, fascists: call this form of ruling whatever you may, but it all begins with the destruction of free speech, the infringement of individual thought.

1984 didn't predict a future. Instead, it warned us of our own roles within the creation of such political systems that seek to control and limit our freedoms. It taught us to think for ourselves, to question, to be skeptical, to seek the truth and use knowledge to inform our decisions. Today though, our own government spews the same rhetoric of which The Party fed to the masses on telescreens. Individual thought and critical thinking are replaced for ignorance and falsehoods deemed fact only to feed the opinions of the self-deluded.

My tattered copy of *1984* sits on my desk, a constant reminder to never be part of the status quo, to always find my voice amongst the cacophony of homogeny. I have always prided myself on my ability to think for myself, to always stick to my principles, even if it alienates me. And that is more important now than it ever has been.

I think back to that day. The roll of the ferry over soft sinking swells, and that young man, a vagabond traveler who lived his life under an Orwellian philosophy that individual thought should never be sold at any price. But what was more important was his exuberance, and how *1984* elicited this response. *1984* inspired our exchange of ideals, our commiseration of beliefs, vigorous debate.

In that moment, I did not feel alone in my ideals. They did not feel radical or rebellious, but normal and thought out. *1984* brought that together, created the conduit between questioning and normalcy. It forced us both to question society and how it is formed, created, and what our places were within its construct.

I hope that young man is still out there. I think of him as John the Baptist, or, to pick a secular character, Johnnie Appleseed. He is traveling right now, sowing the seeds of *1984*, leaving well-read and loved copies for the masses to find, in the hope it will enlighten them in this era that seeks to strip us all of our individualism and suppress our thoughts. In the end, *1984* doesn't tell us how to think or what to think, but encourages us to think. That is the importance of freedom, the ability to think without oppression, because freedom isn't slavery and ignorance isn't strength.

David Jester is a writer, firefighter, paramedic, and directed by wanderlust. He has written for *Atlas Obscura, The Bangor Daily News*, been featured on *Slate.com*, and is a member and regular contributor of Drinkers With Writing Problems out of Chicago. In his free time he drinks cocktails, creates trouble, and analyses culture. You can find my work at dfjester.com.

How *1984* Can Decode Trump's First 100 Days

By Alexander J. Urbelis

Watching me read *1984*, arguably the greatest dystopian novel ever written, in high school, my mother told me that it was a book that everyone should read not just once, but again, every ten years. It certainly deserves a reread right now.

Indeed, dozens of news stories this week have alerted us to surging sales of George Orwell's *1984* since the inauguration and even more so in the wake of Kellyanne Conway's now-infamous "alternative facts" gambit. Most media outlets have reported glibly on the figures, with some going so far as to compare the Amazon best-seller list (where purchases of *1984* have gone up nearly 10,000%) to a "political barometer" before making the obvious parallel between the Orwellian concepts of Newspeak and Doublethink and the words of Conway and actions of White House communications director Sean Spicer.

Yet surprisingly, very few have neither unpacked the full measure of the parallels between Orwell's dystopia and the Trump administration, nor the import of the Trump administration's practices (so far) if left unchecked. As the protagonist of *1984*, Winston Smith, was warned:

"Always, at every moment, there will be the thrill of victory, the sensation of trampling on an enemy who is helpless. If you want a picture of the future, imagine a boot stamping on a human face—forever."

If the sales figures tell us anything, it's that we are right to want a fuller account of the comparisons between literature's most infamous cautionary dystopia and a new American presidential administration.

I believe we are treading into territories more treacherous than even Orwell himself contemplated. We now have a President and an administration in power that expects its own versions of reality and events to be created for it, à la carte, after the fact.

This is not the first time in recent memory that sales of *1984* have spiked. In June 2013, Edward Snowden let the world know the machinations of the US surveillance apparatus were turned not only outward but inward on a massive scale. But this new surge in popularity has a far more pernicious cause: the linguistic assault on, and blatant disregard for, the truth and rational thought by senior Trump administration officials and the President himself.

We are now fighting a battle over who controls the very notion of what is real and fake, true and false. We cannot afford to mince words: President Trump and his staff have used, and will use, lies and deceit to create a false perception of reality that suits their political agenda.

They have espoused as truth unsupportable and untenable falsehoods on a daily basis, and it has become the near-full time responsibility of the media to call out the fictions of the administration. If we do not continue the struggle for basic honesty, we are warned by Orwell that uncorrected lies will be "passed into history and [become] truth."

What *1984* tells us about ourselves

1984 is a menacing tale about the fictional state of Oceania. It exists in a state of continuous and seemingly never-ending war, its institutions are notoriously revisionist and manipulative of public perception with no regard for historical facts or truth. Overseeing law and order and guarding against even minor rebellion is overt and omnipresent government surveillance; and in the seat of power directing all functions of state is Big Brother, a cult of personality demanding of the most intense personal and political loyalty.

For me, however, *1984* has been more than a cautionary tale of dystopia: The concepts, characters and lessons have in a real sense guided me both personally and professionally. My teenage years were spent as a hacker, frequently sneaking into Manhattan from Long Island to attend the infamous 2600 Meetings, an underground monthly gathering of New York's hackers in the lobby of the Citigroup building.

At the center of these meetings was the editor-in-chief of *2600: The Hacker Quarterly*, "Emmanuel Goldstein," whose nom de guerre was taken directly from the principal (and likely fictitious) enemy of the state in *1984.* Emmanuel and I have a friendship spanning nearly 25 years, and I still regularly contribute to his hacker-focused radio show and podcast, "Off the Hook," airing weekly on WBAI in New York. As a teenager, I saw several friends from the circle of 2600 hauled off to prison; their experiences cemented my desire to become a lawyer.

In the midst of my first read of *1984,* my mother surprised my sister and me with a puppy, a beautiful little black mutt abandoned at a groomer's office. This puppy was willful, forceful and seemed always to be plotting against all attempts to exercise authority or dominion over him. He was the embodiment of Orwell's concept of Thoughtcrime, the criminal act of opposing the ruling party, so we named him Winston after Winston Smith in *1984.*

Winston remained steadfastly contrarian and by my side for 16 years, seeing me through high school, college, law school and then real life. When Winston died in 2011, I began volunteering with a local NYC dog rescue, Mighty Mutts, and during one shift I will never forget, the most perfect beagle up for adoption jumped into my lap and refused to leave, as if pronouncing to the world that I was now hers.

When I asked for her name, I could not believe my ears when I was told "Julia," the very name of Winston's counterpart in *1984,* his kindred spirit and fellow outlaw. We adopted Julia immediately, and until she joined Winston over the rainbow bridge earlier this year, she took over his role as a daily reminder of the wisdom of *1984* and the very special place that novel holds in my heart.

Orwell's lessons, cautions and predictions have in my life never been more real and more serious than they are now. Those lessons and parallels merit serious consideration.

Much has been written about Newspeak, the fictional language of Oceania, with its deliberately limited and constantly diminishing vocabulary, and how its assaults on truth and reason parallel Trump administration practices. The idea behind Newspeak is that by reducing vocabulary it is also possible to constrict personal thought and the freedom of expression.

In Orwell's world, there is no such thing as the word "bad," it is instead "ungood." But could this very surface-level comparison between Newspeak and Conway's characterization of Spicer's blatant lies as "alternative facts" really be spurring such resurgence in interest in the *1984*? Of course not. There is more.

In everything from his Cabinet appointments to the rationale for destabilizing executive orders, President Trump appears to have taken a cue directly from *1984*'s fictional ministries, whose purposes are diametrically opposed to their names. Orwell's Ministry of Truth ("Minitrue" in Newspeak), for example, had nothing to do with truth but was responsible for the fabrication of historical facts.

In that vein, President Trump has provided us, in the name of security, with a travel ban on immigrants and refugees from countries whose citizens have caused the terrorism deaths of no Americans, while leaving out countries whose citizens have caused the terrorism deaths of thousands of Americans.

He has provided us with Betsy DeVos, a Secretary of Education who is widely believed to oppose public education, and who promotes the truly Orwellian-sounding concept of "school choice," a plan that seems well-intentioned but which critics complain actually siphons much-needed funds from public to private education institutions.

And we cannot fail to mention that Scott Pruitt — head of the Environmental Protection Agency, which has responsibility to protect health and the environment—who, as Oklahoma attorney general devoted his office to battling the EPA, actively sought deregulation of air pollution requirements, and spearheaded the attack on Obama's efforts to reduce global warming, the Clean Power Plan.

What is truly terrifying is that President Trump and his people refuse to recognize the contradictory nature of their positions, which is the condition perfectly described in *1984* as Doublethink. "[T]o hold simultaneously two opinions which canceled out, knowing them to be contradictory and believing both of them" is Doublethink. And most germane: "To tell deliberate lies while genuinely believing in them, to forget any fact that has become inconvenient, and then, when it becomes necessary again, to draw it back from oblivion for just as long as it is needed" is Doublethink.

Going hand-in-hand with the concept of Doublethink was the notion of Blackwhite: "a loyal willingness to say that black is white when party discipline demands." Blackwhite, however, is more sinister, in that it "means also the ability to believe that black is white ... to know that black is white, and to forget that one has ever believed to the contrary."

We saw this firsthand when President Trump addressed staff members at the CIA. As he recalled his mental impressions of the inauguration crowd, he said, "I looked out, the field was—it looked like a million,

million and a half people." And I do not think he was lying. I believe that President Trump believed this because he had to believe it: The revision of events one day prior to his speech was necessary because it was the only way he could assert legitimacy to control the present moment. The worst, however, is not that Conway and Spicer so easily and willingly followed suit with their own acts of Blackwhite, but that they really believed that we—the media and the people— would in turn do the same.

In a famous passage of *1984*, large crowds gather to denounce Oceania's longstanding rival, Eurasia. Mid-speech, a slip of paper is passed to the speaker, and midsentence, without batting an eyelid, the speaker changes the name of the enemy to Oceania's long-time ally, Eastasia. With a simple act of Blackwhite, foe was changed to friend, and friend to foe.

We are living in this state of flux in real life. Russia was and likely is our nation's fiercest rival, yet as a candidate, President Trump famously stated, "Russia, if you're listening, I hope you're able to find the 30,000 [Clinton] emails that are missing." He praises Putin but states that perhaps he may not actually like him when they meet. WikiLeaks published DNC data alleged to have been obtained by Russian operatives, but the election was not "rigged." A recount would be "ridiculous," yet voter fraud was rampant. Trusted sources of information are "fake news," and somehow Chelsea Manning, WikiLeaks' most notable whistleblower, is now an "ungrateful traitor."

Flying in the face of bipartisan condemnation of his delusional theory of voter fraud, President Trump has now vowed to launch a "major investigation" into the fictional fraudsters that "cost him" the popular vote. With such an Orwellian twist, perhaps we will soon learn that the millions of elusive mystery voters all registered under the name "Emmanuel Goldstein."

One week into Trump's presidency, the parallels with *1984* are more than surface-level, and this portends an ominous future for the United States, regardless of your political persuasion. We among all the species are gifted with language, with thought, with the ability to freely express every singular emotion we experience with sincerity and honesty. We have today what Winston and Julia of Orwell's dystopia lost, fought so hard to reclaim, and failed to achieve: free speech.

At once cautionary and foreboding, certain passages of *1984* eloquently remind us to hold onto the ideals of truth and equality, because simple truths that bind us are stronger than complex lies that divide us:

"It was curious to think that the sky was the same for everybody, in Eurasia or Eastasia as well as here. And the people under the sky were also very much the same—everywhere, all over the world, hundreds or thousands of millions of people just like this, people ignorant of one another's existence, held apart by walls of hatred and lies, and yet almost exactly the same —a people who had never learned to think but were storing up in their hearts and bellies and muscles the power that would one day overturn the world."

Before Winston, my dog, passed away, I promised him that my firstborn son would carry his name. Loving that dog as much as I did, my kind wife allowed me to make good on that promise. Our son's middle name is Winston, and like the Winston and Julia who came before him, for me his name is symbolic of the constant struggle against tyranny and for truth.

I sincerely hope that every newly bought copy of *1984* is read through and through, and, as my mother admonished, read again and again, because that novel shows us that what is at stake right now is nothing short of the legitimacy, confidence and honesty of our republic.

Alexander J. Urbelis is a lawyer and self-described hacker with more than 20 years' experience with information security. He has worked as a graduate fellow in the Office of General Counsel of the Central Intelligence Agency, as a law clerk at the US Court of Appeals for the Armed Forces, and as an associate in the New York and Washington offices of Steptoe & Johnson. He was also information security counsel and chief compliance officer of one of the world's largest luxury conglomerates. He is currently a partner in the Blackstone Law Group and CEO of a separate information security consultancy. Follow him on Twitter @aurbelis.

Big Media is Big Brother
By Mike Siegel, Ph.D, J.D.

George Orwell was prophetic in his capturing of the elements of big government taking control of the lives of its citizens. His notions of perpetual war, unrelenting government surveillance, manipulation of the citizenry, and thought control were concepts not even remotely considered conceivable in a free society such as the United States of America and its foundation in our Constitution.

Of course in 1949, we had just been a major factor in liberating Europe from the throes of Nazi control and could not imagine that *1984*, published in 1949, would play out with its warnings here in America.

Orwell developed the concept of Newspeak, an invented language by government and the notions of "individualism" and "independent thinking" became "Thoughtcrime." The party leader, Big Brother, was a concept and not so much an individual that was primarily created for the building of power for its own sake within the party.

It is instructive to review events of recent years and even days to reflect about the United States and its being caught up in some of these Orwellian notions.

Certainly, the release of NSA information in 2013 by Edward Snowden demonstrates the kind of government intervention and control of the lives of citizens that Orwell described. We learned that every citizen in America was vulnerable to the NSA obtaining telephone records of each of us with a blanket warrant from the Foreign Intelligence Surveillance Court which operates in secret and about which we know very little. The Constitution tells us that the Fourth Amendment requires Probable Cause presented to a judge, with an affidavit before a warrant will be issued.

Views of Snowden vary with passion and intensity, but what we learned from his actions is that the Fourth Amendment protection of our privacy, and that of our papers, was treated with disregard by the Court. Clearly, there was no probable cause for millions of Americans to have their telephone records invaded in clear violation of the standard created by the Founders of this nation.

We then had the Associated Press and James Rosen of Fox News intimidated by the Justice Department under Barack Obama and Eric Holder. Again, the Constitution makes it clear that a free press is to be protected and Thomas Jefferson went so far as to say that given a choice between a strong central government and no free press and no central government and a free press, he would take the latter over the former.

His point was simple. The free press is the auditor of government to hold it accountable to the people. When government interferes with that freedom, it is a move toward what Orwell described as Newspeak, trying to control the message to have government seen in its most favorable light. In other words, it can do no wrong.

We have seen police departments around the country collecting license plate numbers of automobiles to build a database for their own use. Again, the police need reasonable suspicion or probable cause to interfere with citizens, and it is therefore arguable that randomly having a police agency take photos of license plates with justification is a further erosion of individual protection.

The mainstream media in America are part and parcel of what Orwell warned us about when it comes to thought control efforts. We know that 96% of journalists donated to Hilary Clinton in the last election. We know that well over 95% of federal employees did the same.

Here we have the foundation for a dangerous control by government and media that do its bidding. Independent studies have shown that the reporting about President Donald Trump since he ran for office until now has been overwhelmingly negative. A simple review of how the mainstream media treated the Benghazi issue, Fast and Furious, the political abuse of the IRS, the numerous times that President Obama was rejected by the Supreme Court in a number of his actions and we see the pattern.

Had those acts been carried out by a Republican, it would have been a relentless campaign by the media to condemn and punish the wrongdoers. Not so with the last administration.

When the police actions that were condemned by the Obama administration later turned out to exonerate those officers, the press was meek and mild in covering that overreach by the administration. Again, had this been a Republican administration, the coverage would have been dramatically different.

How do we know? Just observe how the mainstream media are covering the alleged relationship between the Trump campaign and Russia. James Comey, FBI Director, was readily willing to publicly state that there is an ongoing investigation of this alleged link, yet there is no evidence at all of this assertion. At the same time, he was unwilling to publicly state that there is another ongoing investigation of the leak of secured information or of the perpetrator of the release of General Michael Flynn's conversation with the Russian Ambassador and other leaked information. These are potentially crimes that have as much as 10 year prison sentences. Why would he publicly acknowledge the investigation leaving a cloud over the Trump administration yet not do the same with an investigation that may cast doubt on government employees apparently intending to do harm to this administration? And, where are the mainstream media in all of this? Predictably covering the alleged Russian connection like a glove and reporting almost nothing on the criminally leaked information attempting to sabotage the Trump administration. So much for the fair and balanced media.

The point of these examples is that we have in America the symptom of what Orwell warned us about. There is a strong cabal between the mainstream media and the political left to control the message, eliminate opposing views, and thereby control though through "Newspeak."

Perhaps the most troubling aspect of this situation is the repeated series of acts of violence by students on the left at college and university campuses. At the University of California at Berkeley and Middlebury College as the most recent examples, students literally shut down speakers and caused violent damage to property and injury to people.

We saw organized groups during the campaign physically block Trump supporters from getting to rallies.

Recently there was a series of rallies supporting President Trump across the country and in at least one instance, anti-Trump activists created violent confrontation with this group.

This movement that wants to eliminate the opposing point of view is precisely what Orwell described.

Fortunately, to this point, the American people showed their sense of independence in the last election and rejected that kind of control.

That gives us hope and meaningful inspiration that we can avoid what Orwell described and maintains the greatness of our Constitution.

Mike Siegel, a talk host with decades of experience, goes beyond the slanted coverage of the mainstream media and covers the real issues of the day. His conservative-libertarian views dominate his approach to the issues. Whether it is potential constitutional violations or lack of leadership by the President, Mike Siegel uses his penetrating analysis to get the real issues to his audience. His ratings and revenue success over the years demonstrates the compelling and energetic component of his programs. He has motivated his audience to action when he led a national campaign to stop a 51% pay raise in Congress; a campaign to hold Exxon accountable for the Valdez oil spill that led to Congress passing a law requiring double hull oil tankers by the year 2010 and many other issues in which his audiences have had an activist role.

As a former practicing attorney, Mike brings his legal analysis to public issues as well, giving his audience the kind of coverage the audience seeks.

Mike Siegel will tell you what he thinks without qualification. He will support those views with solid analysis. As a pragmatist who finds solutions to problems, audiences have gravitated to his programs over the years.

Mike Siegel's real world experience as a public school teacher in Newark, New Jersey; Professor of Communication at Emerson College in Boston; Consultant to a Drug Rehabilitation Program in Boston; Communication Consultant to Business and Industry have given him a breadth and depth of experience that he brings to his programs.

Mike holds a Ph.D. in Communication from the University of Utah and a J.D. from Nova University Law Center.

Controlling The Present:
How *1984* Predicted 'Alternative Facts' and 'Fake News'

By Marc W. Polite

George Orwell's *1984* has resurfaced as a text of interest in our current American political reality. With the ascendance of Donald Trump as 45th president of these United States, it seems as though the electorate in this country has reached back into history to deal with the problems of the 21st Century. Successfully campaigning on racism, misogyny and xenophobia, to many the Trump Administration feels more like a regime than the result of a democratic process. This being the case, it is no major surprise that people are returning to the classic novel that was a denunciation of 20th Century totalitarianism.

In our political discourse soon after the inauguration of Donald Trump, a very curious term slipped into the lexicon. Counselor to the President Kellyanne Conway, in defense of White House Press Secretary Sean Spicer giving out false statements about the size of the crowds at the inauguration, said that he was giving out "alternative facts." Not lies, but "alternative facts." The term Orwellian applies here aptly.

In the novel *1984*, Winston Smith worked in the Records Department in the Ministry of Truth. It was his job to alter and update records from the past to fit the ever-changing dictates of Big Brother, the unquestionable leader of Oceania. The department took great care in collaborating with the destruction of all written vestiges of the past, so there will be no contradiction. "Who controls the past, controls the future... who controls the present, controls the past." This was one of the Ingsoc Party slogans. Entire lives were made up, and stories concocted. There is your precedent for "fake news."

Today, although not willing to go nearly as far, we have officials who utter untruths and ignore reality when it doesn't suit their talking points. The Two-Minutes Hate depicted in *1984* has been extended to a 24-hour news cycle where the public is bombarded with information. We live in a "post facts" era, where people don't dig beyond headlines, and aren't encouraged to. Historical context does not matter, and inconvenient truths go down the "memory hole" of the mainstream media by omission. Science is denied, and accusation of foreign meddling in elections amounts to damning evidence. Warm late February days are regarded as wonders, and in the same breath climate change is said to be overblown. In response to all of the leaks of 2016, came the Countering Disinformation and Propaganda Act.

In late February, the Trump Administration banned the *New York Times* and CNN from a White House briefing. While no one was "vaporized" as dissenters were in Orwell's classic novel, the freedom of the press became a privilege that could be revoked at the whim of those in power. This reality puts us all in a dangerous position. Here we are, in an era where the truth is secondary to the political agenda of the day. Where we cannot even ask how we arrived here politically without the danger of inflaming the partisan sentiments of one side or another. The old axiom goes that "The first casualty of war is truth." Considering our current predicament, this appears to hold. How long until we are asked to believe that $2 + 2 = 5$?

Marc W. Polite is the winner of a Best Blog Commentary Award from the New York Association of Black Journalists. He writes on issues concerning history, labor, and technology. Mr. Polite is the founder and Editor-in-Chief of Polite On Society, which won a Best Black Blog Award from the Historical Black Press Foundation for its social commentary, political analysis and literary reviews. He is the author of *Everything To Learn, Nothing To Teach*, a collection of essays on social issues, contemporary politics, and some of his personal experiences.

Trump is not Orwellian: He is the Distractor-in-Chief
By Matt Bai

"Never use a metaphor, simile, or other figure of speech which you are used to seeing in print," George Orwell once wisely admonished his fellow writers. So you have to wonder what Orwell would make of all these commentators who have worn out the term "Orwellian" during these first weeks of the Trump administration, leading to a spike in sales of *1984* and *Animal Farm.*

I'm glad for this boomlet, since Orwell was a singular voice on 20th Century authoritarianism and how we write about it; the brilliant essay from which I took the above quote, "Politics and the English Language," is something every aspiring writer should study. ("The great enemy of clear language is insincerity," Orwell observed, which is probably the most essential insight into political debate—or the craft of writing generally—that you will ever hear.)

But Orwell's dark prophecy isn't actually the one that best explains the moment we're living through right now. And to the extent that we focus on fears of statist mind control and mass disinformation, we may miss the subtler thing that's really going on.

Here I turn again to the late Neil Postman, whose classic critique of mid-80s culture *Amusing Ourselves to Death*, is as relevant today as it was then. In his foreword, Postman compared Orwell's vision of fascist repression with the trivial, substanceless society envisioned by Aldous Huxley in his 1932 novel *Brave New World.*

In Huxley's vision, Postman wrote, "no Big Brother is required to deprive people of their autonomy, maturity and history. As he saw it, people will come to love their oppression, to adore the technologies that undo their capacities to think."

It's worth hearing a bit more of Postman's comparison: "What Orwell feared were those who would ban books. What Huxley feared was that there would be no reason to ban a book, for there would be no one who wanted to read one. ... Orwell feared that truth would be concealed from us. Huxley feared that truth would be drowned in a sea of irrelevance."

As it happens, in 1949, just after the publication of *1984,* Huxley drew much the same contrast in a letter to his countryman Orwell. Much as he liked Orwell's book, he suggested that tyrannical governments would soon abandon "boot-on-the-face" tactics in favor of "animal magnetism and hypnotism." Cable TV had yet to be invented.

Brave New World, which I went back and reread last week, is a trippy little book, and Huxley was a more transparent polemicist—and less of a storyteller—than Orwell. His vision of a genetically engineered populace sedated by sex, movies, drugs and golf, to the point where no one can focus on anything long enough to be alarmed by the soulless state of society, is a bit too fantastical even now.

And yet there's something bracing, given today's political debate, about the way Mustapha Mond, the state controller, warns his charge: "Every discovery in pure science is potentially subversive; even science must sometimes be treated as a possible enemy." Or about the way he defends inequality: "The optimum population is modeled on the iceberg—eight-ninths below the water line, one-ninth above."

Substitute YouTube and smartphones and the Real Housewives of Wherever for the free love and free narcotics Huxley envisioned, and his parable seems disturbingly relevant. Mustapha Mond would not feel horribly out of place in an administration stocked with climate-change deniers and billionaires.

President Trump doesn't strike me as a very convincing Big Brother. You don't go out of your way to alienate security services if you're considering the imposition of a police state. You don't put Reince Priebus in charge of the White House if you're ramping up for world domination.

In some ways, though, Trump is the perfect embodiment of a Huxleyan culture, endlessly distracted by the superficial or the spectacular. He doesn't want to control what you think—only what you think *about*, which is him. He cares that you're watching the performance, and it doesn't matter whether you watch because you love it or because you find it too grossly compelling to look away.

I've written before that Trump is an emotional extremist, not an ideological one. His gift is for channeling the passion in an audience, for provoking adoration or outrage or whatever's most visceral.

Why does the president of the United States stoop

to accusing Chuck Schumer of faking his tears? Because low is entertaining, and entertaining is the way he maintains control. Changing the conversation before you can even remember what the last conversation was about—this is what Trump does better than anyone alive.

And the danger here is that the constant trivia can too easily distract us from decisions that have deadly serious consequences. Like Huxley's Alphas and Betas, we can be lulled into thinking that the ephemeral is all there is.

Since Trump took office less than two weeks ago, we've been mesmerized by spectacle. There was the attack on the Park Service for not backing up the president on the size of his inauguration crowds ... and the unprompted allegations over voter fraud ... and the dramatic rollout of his crackdown on Muslim immigrants, which even the White House didn't seem to understand.

Somehow Trump managed to manufacture controversy by pointedly leaving Jews out of a statement about the Holocaust. Somehow he figured out how to turn a Supreme Court nomination into a primetime special more like the NFL draft.

It's not as if the immigration ban and a seat on the high court aren't important—they really are. But at the same time, the public is less focused on Trump's decision, made with no theatrical flourish, to give Steve Bannon, his liaison to the world of white nationalists, a permanent seat on the National Security Council's principals committee—rather than allotting it to, say, the chairman of the Joint Chiefs.

There's not so much discussion about Trump's

prompt withdrawal from the Asian trade pact, which a lot of Democrats applauded but which has grave implications for our economic power in the region. Likewise on Trump's proposed tariffs on exports, which could lead us quickly into an all-out trade war.

There's not much focus on what's happening now in the Middle East, where Israel, emboldened by Trump's rhetoric, is about to vastly accelerate settlements in the occupied territories. The public isn't buzzing about the imminent dismantling of the EPA.

The challenge for all of us—and especially those of us in the media—is to differentiate between distraction and the more permanent reality. We can't let ourselves be perpetually amused into economic or global crisis.

A performer as talented as Trump can do that, and there might be nothing Orwellian about it.

Matt Bai is the national political columnist for Yahoo News. Before that, he was the chief political correspondent for the *New York Times Magazine*, where he covered three presidential campaigns. His latest book, *All The Truth Is Out: The Week Politics Went Tabloid*, was named one of 2014's best books by Amazon.com and NPR. He lives with his family in Bethesda, Maryland.

Why Orwell's Sudden Best-Seller *1984* is More Applicable to Obama Than Trump

By Jay Strongman

One of the most bizarre aspects of President Trump's first few weeks in office is that a book written by an Englishman back in 1949 has suddenly become a bestselling novel in the America of 2017.

The book is George Orwell's dystopian classic *1984* and, without any hint of irony, liberals are hailing the book's warning about the extremes of big government as a primer on what to expect from Trump and his administration.

A cursory glance at mainstream news outlets or at the trending topics on social media shows that President Trump's executive actions so far have convinced his detractors that the government of the USA has overnight turned into the kind of brutal dictatorship portrayed in *1984*.

Sales of the novel have skyrocketed and it has just been announced that an acclaimed British stage adaptation of the novel will transfer to Broadway in June.

This abrupt switch from the government being seen as a wise and benign institution (so long as it was under control of the Democrats) to becoming a wicked and authoritarian one (as in Orwell's novel) miraculously happened only once Trump was sworn in.

A recent review of the book on Amazon sums up the emotions and fears that have seemingly engulfed a large part of the country since the inauguration: "I first read this book as a teenager, and there was a great deal of discussion about the book. Did we really think that life would be as totalitarian and regimented in *1984* as the book predicted? For most of us, no. We realized most would be alive in that year, and we had no fear. Now, in 2017, the fear is here. *1984,* the book is in the top ten booksellers this week. Why? Fascism [sic] is upon us."

The notion that America has suddenly been transformed into a dystopian world of Big Brother and Big Government also roiled the *Huffington Post*. They informed nervous readers not only how much like *1984* Trump's administration already was but also that Orwell's essay "Politics and the English Languag*e*" was even more relevant to Trump's America*:* "*1984* is a classic novel that asks an important question: How far could an authoritarian state go? But "Politics and the English Language" tells us where we are right now. And that, unfortunately, is just as frightening, if not more."

Quite how anything could be more frightening than the totalitarian nightmare described in *1984* is not something that *Huff Post* cares to tell us, but apparently Trump's America is now worse than anything experienced under Stalin's Soviet Union which was Orwell's inspiration for his depiction of life under Big Brother.

One of Trump's "Doublespeak" crimes was apparently saying that he wanted to return law and order to the inner cities—what he was actually doing by saying that was (according to the *Huff Post*) hiding "the evidence that people of color are treated worse by police than white people." Other liberal media mouthpieces carry similar somewhat twisted warnings of the parallels between the book and life under Trump.

And Timothy Snyder, a history professor at Yale University, referenced the book as required reading, kindly giving us 20 top tips on resisting a "repressive state" including the somewhat overly hysterical rhetoric of point 19: "Be as courageous as you can. If none of us is prepared to die for freedom, then all of us will die in unfreedom."

Of course the great irony is that none of the people currently quoting Orwell over Trump's Executive Orders were that bothered when President Obama did the same thing during his administration.

In fact the liberal media and his supporters cheered Obama on to ignore Congress and to use his pen more often to pass the progressive agenda that they favored. Hollywood liberal Gwyneth Paltrow spoke for many on the progressive side when she famously gushed at an Obama fundraiser in 2014 that, "It would be wonderful if we were able to give this man all of the power that he needs to pass the things that he needs to pass."

Those who are just discovering *1984* seem naively unaware that Orwell's fictional spirit-crushing future was a warning against Communism and the unbridled power of an over-reaching government. Trump, for all his myriad faults, seems more concerned with deregulation and taking power away from central government control than building it up.

It was Obama, not Trump, who weaponized the IRS to take down his political opponents and who used the 1917 Espionage Act to prosecute more government whistleblowers than all the previous administrations put together. But none of that unduly bothers today's new liberal Orwell readers.

Another aspect of *1984* that has seemingly gone unnoticed amongst its sudden glut of contemporary fans is the cult of personality described in the book. Big Brother is everywhere, smiling down from huge billboards and leading his people on the path to salvation.

Strangely, the Big Brother comparison didn't seem to bother those on the Democrat side back in 2009 when school children were filmed creepily chanting *"Mmm, mmm, mmm, Barak Hussein Obama"* or when the erstwhile President Obama informed us in 2006 that his selection as the Democrat presidential nominee was "the moment the oceans stopped rising and the world began to heal."

The idea that Big Brother knows all and knows what's best for us also didn't worry progressives when Michelle Obama promised Americans that, "Barack will never allow you to go back to your lives as usual, uninvolved, uninformed." See, Barack knew best and only he can could have stopped you from being uninvolved and uninformed.

Sarcasm aside, America today is nothing like Orwell's *1984*—but the point is that dictatorships of the kind that *1984* shows us don't happen overnight. They develop with the government being given more and more power over our lives until it controls every aspect of our existence—from how much soda pop we're permitted to drink, to what we're allowed to say and think.

And if you don't complain about government abuse when your team is in power, you can't be taken seriously when the next team takes over and uses similar abuses against your side. As George Washington reputedly said, "Government is not reason, it is not eloquence,—it is force! Like fire, it is a dangerous servant, and a fearful master."

Washington had no idea of the horrors that centralized governments would later unleash upon the world but both he and Orwell (who saw those horrors in his lifetime) realized the dual nature of government.

1984 is a stark warning against totalitarianism and what happens when we cede absolute power to authority. Using Orwell's masterpiece merely to inaccurately score political points between Red and Blue and to stir up fear and anger both does a great writer a grave disservice and dilutes an extremely important message.

Jay Strongman was born and raised in southern England. He is a renowned international DJ and a respected commentator on popular and underground culture. Like many of his generation, Jay was heavily influenced by the American TV shows, movies and music that permeated British culture in the 1960s and 70s. That love of mid-20th Century Americana led him to starting London's first neo-rockabilly clothing store, "Rock-A-Cha," in 1979 and fronting a rockabilly band called the El-Trains the same year. He started his DJ career in London in the mid-1980s and his pioneering mix of music led to him becoming one of the first DJs-as-popstars gigging across the globe from Tokyo to Toronto, New York to Sweden, Los Angeles to Rio de

Janeiro and all over Europe. In 1988 he became the first-ever Western DJ to play a warehouse party in the then-Soviet Union and was also the DJ on the first British Rap tour of then-communist East Germany in 1989.

Jay was fashion editor for *Mixmag* magazine in the 1990s and provided music for fashion shows by Vivienne Westwood, Michiko Koshino, Milan Fashion Week and LEVIS amongst others. He also proved the only DJ choice to provide the music soundtrack for the Victoria & Albert Museum's acclaimed "Street Style" exhibition where he mixed together 50 years of dance music—from 1940s swing to modern house.

Besides his 30-plus year career as a DJ, Jay has also been a regular writer on music and popular culture for such publications as the *Face Magazine, The Sunday Times, i-D Magazine, Soul Underground* and *Vogue*. He has had two coffee table art books published: *Tiki Mugs—Cult Artifacts of Polynesian Pop* (Korero Books) and the highly acclaimed *Steampunk—The Art of Victorian Futurism* (Korero Books). And in 2016 his first novel was published—a noir detective story set in the Los Angeles of the 1950s called *Ritual of The Savage.*

Jay currently divides his time DJ'ing both in his newly adopted homeland of Southern California and back in his first love, London Town. He also writes on popular culture for *Heat Street* e-magazine and is now working on a sequel to *Ritual*, a partially autobiographical story about a DJ during the hedonistic 1980s, and a sci-fi fantasy titled *Martian Eye.*

1984: The Facts on the Ground are Emotions

By Alan Saly

The facts are what we say they are. That's probably the most enduring idea that one takes from *1984*—and one that has come to permeate modern life. Spin has always been an acceptable business strategy. You cherry pick what's good about your product and accentuate what's bad about your competition. But then you have an impartial authority, like the government or *Consumer Reports*—that comes in and truly separates the facts from the falsehoods and the exaggerations. In Orwell's *1984*, there is no impartial authority that is bound to find the facts. Instead, the government manipulates the facts—distorting them beyond recognition.

Yet facts about human behavior are different from historical or scientific fact—which is why Winston Smith clings to the idea that there is a thread leading back into the past that he can follow to understand why things are the way they are in the present. The ways people feel about things changes, even as the facts remain the same. Emotional realizations are the most powerful motivators of human behavior. When Winston Smith feels love for

Big Brother in the famous closing lines of *1984*, the facts of the world around him haven't changed. It's his reaction to them that has changed. So the job of the opinion makers around us is to conjure emotions from the facts, because it's in the emotional connection that the man or woman is changed.

1984 shows that the creation of false facts is a dictatorial regime's necessary tool to powerfully manipulate emotions, which in turn makes it possible to change political realities. As a labor union activist, I see this played out on websites all over the Internet. Probably the most used strategy is to combine false fact with actual facts, trusting that the reader — who wants quick and easy answers — won't take the time to research them.

A website like unionfacts.com presents financial expenditures taken from public reports about labor unions and then portrays those expenditures as a rip-off of the union worker. Nowhere is there an attempt to detail the amazing bang for the buck that union members have gotten for their dues investments over the years. But the real point of the site, just as is shown in the final pages of *1984*, is to create powerful emotions about unions— in this case, anger at the alleged misuse of funds, and disgust at the union "fat cats" who are allegedly using the money for personal gain. Because it's the emotions that really move the people, not an understanding of the facts.

All echo chambers are fundamentally alike, because they exist to limit facts and to shield members from the inconvenient ones they don't like. In *1984*, there is only one echo chamber—the one created and maintained by the State. It uses fake facts to channel emotions—the hatred against Emmanuel Goldstein or whichever power Oceania is currently fighting. In the United States of America, there are quite a few of these echo chambers—yet all of them can be profitably compared to one another. Mostly, people are familiar with Fox News on the one hand and MSNBC on the other, not to mention the comedy sites that purvey incisive "fake news," which often turns into real news. There are better examples, where facts are more thoroughly repudiated.

Dylan Roof's murderous rampage in a black church in Charleston, South Carolina, was set off by continued exposure to racist websites that presented false facts about black on white crime, especially about the allegedly overwhelming numbers of rapes of white women. "They rape 100 white women a day," Roof says in a taped interview with his interrogator, Michael Stansbury. Just a few minutes on the Internet reveals this to be false or misleading. Just as a courtroom oath obligates one to speak "the truth, the whole truth, and nothing but the truth," anyone who really wants to be armed with the facts will recognize that facts about human behavior are complex, often qualified by other facts, and have a way of changing over time. The "whole truth" requires a willingness not to be intellectually lazy, to research carefully. Roof's echo chamber, however, wasn't interested in the whole truth. Instead, it put forward false or misleading facts to incite emotions—in his case, murderous rage. Emotions are the currency of action. They make people march, volunteer, contribute money, and sacrifice themselves for good or bad reasons.

The climate change denying echo chamber is another example of how facts are limited and controlled. Disputing facts that are becoming clearer and clearer as climate change advances is only possible because it is linked to a strong emotional signal that doesn't change. The latest wrinkle among the deniers—admitting that climate change is taking place but stating that it isn't being caused by human activity—reveals the heart of it. Admitting that we are the cause of massive changes in the earth system is in some way an attack on my right to pollute and extract, to use my property and my resources in any way I see fit. It's dis-empowering, offensive and limiting. That makes me angry and determined to protect my rights—the "facts" be damned.

Conspiracy theorists have perhaps the most well-known set of insulating, fact-resistant bubbles, as do the religious cultists who declare the end of the world for a particular date, only to adjust the facts when that date comes and goes. No amount of careful parsing of the evidence will convince a believer in the theory that the Twin Towers weren't destroyed by aircraft that his facts are wrong, and again that's because of the emotional resonance of what he believes. For such a believer, the need to believe that what appears to be truth to the general public is instead false, is intense. That's because the belief that one has special and unique knowledge is very gratifying and motivating.

Any echo chamber that suppresses the facts—even to a small degree—risks irrelevancy at the same time as it boosts the emotional intensity that infects its followers—a dangerous combination. The basic assumption—we are always right, they are always wrong—is profoundly limiting and destructive.

As mentioned above, the real horror of *1984* is

that there is only one echo chamber—an overriding, powerful message purveyed by the State, which individuals have limited power to resist. Ripping the lid off the continuing debates over the merits of one echo chamber over another is the depiction of *1984*'s O'Brien as a self-conscious manipulator of the facts who knows exactly what he is doing and the price paid by the public—which he is indifferent to. That portrayal unmasks those who lead and create the false fact infrastructure of our contemporary echo chambers as responsible actors who are determined not to be held accountable for what they are doing.

One thing that George Orwell did not foresee was digital technology, which makes manipulation of the facts much easier than ever before—in the sense that images and video and audio recordings can now easily be modified and altered. Donald Trump has pre-figured this danger by openly doubting the truth conveyed by respected news outlets. Widespread surveillance by our government also begs the question of whether any kind of digital media, in any form, is actually the genuine article.

What matters so much to us in the drama of *1984* are the emotions of Winston Smith and of Julia. Winston is appalled at how his emotions are being manipulated by the regime, and finds in Julia the inspiration to feel differently. His job, of course, is to conceal and manipulate facts, and because he does this, he knows how ephemeral the state-created false facts are. Yet he is desperately searching for the truth—for facts that he can orient his life around. He longs for a world where facts are truly honest and objective.

So do we.

Alan Saly is the Director of Print and Electronic Publications at Transport Workers Union Local 100 in New York City. He has been a union activist for over 20 years, with other unions including Emergency Medical Services Local 2507 of DC 37. He attended marches at Occupy Wall Street with members of TWU Local 100 and assisted in organizing OWS events. His family emigrated from Hungary, which experienced much of the post and pre-war impact of extreme right-wing totalitarianism, as well as Stalinism. This informed his reading of *1984.* His views do not represent the official views of TWU Local 100.

Sure, It's "1984" Again—And I Know It
By Perry Brass

It's "1984" again, and I know it, both as a writer and a person. People are always doing the "best thing for you," or the *worst* thing, while offering you those famous choices of no choices, offering you what I call the "You can always—" alternative. As in, with Facebook censuring me constantly, "You can always do without Facebook." Sure, now approaching two billion members, Facebook's a mega-country in its own right. Or, facing censorship problems from Amazon, "You can always do without Amazon." That's great for a writer. Do without the world's largest retailer and bookseller, after it's decimated the country's independent bookstores.

Or better: "You can always stop writing."

I knew things were going to be fucked up in this way. I've written about it in my own science fiction and futurist novels for the last 20-something years. But that doesn't mean I like it. Like any writer, it doesn't mean I enjoy being right—and, unfortunately, it also didn't take a genius to figure it out. You just had to connect all the dots, even some that were way off the page. Dots like:

All of us now living in our Trumpian Universe are experiencing a "perfect storm" of slowly compressing social defecation hitting us smack behind the head and solidifying. First, we had the Twin Horses of the Apocalypse: Political Correctness on the Right—all those people going out to save "the little babies" and turning the choice to terminate a pregnancy into a capital offense (quoting the Beloved Donald during his campaign, "there's got to be punishment somehow") as well as kissing up to the billionaires while screaming about "elitism" at the same time. And Political Correctness on the Left, when any assertion of truth—*damn*, what an outmoded term!—regarding the socio/economic/political hell we're in is branded as, you got it, "racist, classist, and fascist."

In other words, the "minorities" in many places are now a *majority*, and you can talk all you want to about "Black Lives Matter," but in our Big Bank-and-Wall-Street-dominated, hard-as-rocks, *yuge* dollar-choked class system—where you have to take out a mortgage to eat dinner out with friends, and millions of people are basically three paychecks away from living on the street—they *don't*.

We are also now living in the height of what I term Ronald Reagan's great legacy to the world: Narcissistic Capitalism. That means claiming the glories of free market enterprise as an "expression of your own deepest self."

When this idea first popped up, I thought, these *shits* have got to be kidding? Reagan's young, idealistic and deluded followers were asserting that Business was *now* the culminating Art Form of the 20th Century. Forget those old-fashioned "elitist" cultural pursuits we once all knew and loved—the *real* Art Form became the Business Plan. Doing a "great" Business Plan was like writing a major novel, or a piece of poetry; it was as satisfying to produce as a superb painting, or a timeless movie.

Andy Warhol said, "Business is Art and Art is Business," but he was goofing on us. These turds were taking it seriously. Suddenly "B" schools were flooded with applications. Business is currently the overwhelming major of most American college undergraduates, and business language has become the *lingua franca* of life. After I published my guide *The Manly Art of Seduction*, a 20-something kid asked me, "What do you think is the ultimate 'deal breaker' in a relationship? I think it's smoking, but sometimes it's that a guy just doesn't have a real job."

I had to stop for a second. What the hell was he talking about? The heart doesn't have "deal breakers." Like most things human, it simply doesn't want to break.

Business lingo has contracted all human interactions; it is the Newspeak of our time. There is "Appropriate" and "Inappropriate," and you are very quickly aware of who decides what is what. My favorites among the deciders are the gym-sculpted hedge-fund laddies in "informal black." They cut your balls off with their high-priced informality: the $2,000 black Versace pants; the $500 black Italian T-shirt; the $1,000 black lizard-skin belt, and, just to add a bit of fuck-you street pizazz, a cool pair of pristine black Nikes. They remind me of crocodiles crawling up on dry land, blood oozing out of their teeth, but they are certainly aware of what the *Brand* is.

They know the strength of it, and its weakness.

Because the Brand is everything. The Brand is *God*. And you'd better have one of your own: Your own little Brand and your own little God.

Now—more than anything—you're not a citizen. You're not even a human. You *are* a Brand. You're your own Brand, and that Brand must be promoted, pushed out onto the national stage, and given its God-given right to succeed more than anyone else. In fact, any *thing* else is an offense: it's like rape. When your Brand is not universally recognized and respected, certainly the way Ivanka Trump's Brand has got to be, the whole System is suspect. That means the *System* needs to be questioned, and with some amount of effort, but *not* work (remember: "work" is for losers), jettisoned—dismantled piece by terrifying piece.

In other words, let's destroy the System, but definitely not the Brand.

You have an inalienable right to your Brand. It goes with Life, Liberty, and the Pursuit of Happiness. It was established at birth, which is why abortion is no longer even a possible choice. Abortion means you are killing off all those cute future Brands along with the little babies, too.

(That the welfare of children is definitely not as important as saving "the little babies" means—OK, we get it. It absolutely proves that fetuses, too, have a right to their own Brand.)

You are known by (and for) your Brand, in the same manner that you exist because of what you buy: It's your own real *authentic* identity.

As a starring member of the American "consumerate" (remember, we no longer have the electorate, just the *consumerate*), you're entitled to everything. It's a simple formula—you are identified, kept alive and desirable as the receiver of everything, because everything will be offered to you on the Silver Platter of your own endlessly *replenishable* credit. This means that as a functioning part of the great White People's Banking System (to which every molecule of you is in hock), you've got nothing to worry about. Because the "real" business of the entire country, piling up ever-higher credit card, educational, housing, and health debts, must be kept going.

The idea of it stopping it is too terrifying. We came close in 2008, when all the failing Big Banks and their bankers had to circle their wagons around themselves and crush anyone who wasn't on their side.

But as a "starring" member of the consumerate even the *idea* that you can't have it all revolts you. You are *not* what you eat, you *are* what you buy: I hope you got that. You may be standing on a ledge on the 95th floor but as long as you don't look down at all those poor people down on the street, you'll be fine!

Remember—all those TV ads for Porsches, Infinities, classy "Jag-u-wars," and endless youth, perfect skin and Hilton vacations... all those Macy's "One Day!" sales; all those 57th Street luxury shops with more Security guards in them than customers—well, they are *all* there for you.

So what the fuck's wrong with you that you can't have it all?

It should be coming out of your asshole every moment. None of the consumerate should ever stop binge consuming because, ah, if we do, the whole *System* falls apart.

It's unpatriotic! It's Third World! It means that if you have that piss-poor idea that the consumerate can't absorb any more shit, you should be at the very least chemically castrated. I mean I admit it: the idea does hit everybody at some point—just how many more *schmattas* from H & M can anybody buy? How much more McDonalds' can anybody eat? How many more luxury cars can anybody drive?

What would happen if we realized suddenly, all of us, that the most absolute "luxury" would be having *time* for yourself without the usual soul-eating anxiety and insecurity attached to it?

OK. Just keep those reservations under lock and key. Don't spread them around, because if you do, like Winston Smith in Orwell's novel, it will be very bad for you. It means you are starting to think on your own, and that is never tolerated even in our ruthlessly "tolerant" world.

After all, you *should* have it all.

In one of my futurist novels, set in the year 2075, I explained that every new product had to be designed to set off "the release element"—the complete shopping orgasm. It's got to give you what other human beings no longer can. It's got to make you say: *I gotta have it!* And if I can't, I'm going to have a fit— and elect some boob like Donald Trump president, because only *Donald* knows how much I want it!

Which means to get it, I've got to have a "real" job. That is, an actual position that pays me more than most of the humanoid semi-robots around me, the ones still clinging desperately to the "gig" economy, the ones with no future at all.

But—suppose I can't get a job? I'll still want

everything because it's the only *thing* I'm capable of accepting. (Now this is where things get sticky, and even Donald walks out of the room—)

Because the truth is, I can no longer accept my *real* self.

Because... well, there just isn't one. The fucking truth is, I don't have a *real* self; it's been washed away in a constant commercial bath of "Self-Esteem."

"Self-Esteem" started to emerge at the same time that Narcissistic Capitalism did, and it's now a major industry. We have several generations of kids who are bloated with it. They don't have a *real* self, one that they can separate from our stampeding shopping malls of Narcissistic Capitalism, where every day is Black Friday. But they do definitely have "Self-Esteem."

"Self-Esteem" is presently taught in endless classes and workshops. There are specialists in it who will tell you that "Self-Esteem" is the birthright of all humans, and that any form of real critical thinking will be despised and exposed as "Anti-Self-Esteem." If you don't believe Beyoncé is the world's greatest pop star, you are "Anti-Self-Esteem," because so many people adore her and being critical of her is—well, against "Self-Esteem." Her millions of fans would like to be her—or at least *buy* her—and they have every right to feel that way because it affects their "Self-Esteem." They want to organically absorb that twinkly aura of Super-Stardom that surrounds her, until they, too, become Beyoncé.

And the truth is, with enough "Self-Esteem," they can.

It will come in a little bottle that you can buy at Victoria's Secret, along with that Great Celestial iPhone where the genii of Siri appears and talks to you so privately and intimately that you will forget momentarily how *alone* you really are.

All of this is sold with "Self-Esteem."

I know you want that instead of sex, because *real* sex has become so "dirty"—i.e., meaning loaded with consequences that go against the P.C.ism of the Corporate State—that it has become more of a turn-off than that moment when you pull out your wallet, hand over your Platinum Amex card, and then cum all over yourself when what you want, what you've *got* to have, is handed to you in a classy shopping bag equipped with real rope handles. (Those rope handles are the most *genuine* thing in the transaction. People have been known to hang themselves with them.)

Real sex, though, easily segues into "sexual harassment," and you know you can't have that. We can't have spontaneous attraction anymore, only suspicions of harassment. Therefore, stick to shopping. That's where the real safe "anonymous"-sex-with-no-fluids-exchange is happening, between you and people you'll never get to meet. And, that's also why shopping over the Internet will never replace salivating over a good-looking guy at the tie counter at Barney's.

I was told by Gupta on the "Amazon Marketing team" that I cannot, under any circumstances, advertise my books on Amazon's site because of their covers, and/or content. "There are people," Gupta informed me, "who will find offense in your work. They will see that it is either sexually or religiously offensive."

Amazon, which in the last century was for the "little guy," has instituted "Global Community

Guidelines" for promoting books. This means that anyone, anywhere, can be offended by something in print, and therefore only the most genial, inoffensive, and bland material is now of real "Amazon quality." Since there is no way to be "discovered" anymore online in the thickening morass of product glut in our faceless but always Facebooked world, I will soon sink into a stinking rut worse than death: Total Anonymity. I have experienced the same thing on Facebook, which also has instituted "Global Community Guidelines" of its own.

It's painful.

I have gone from being an Amazon bestseller in the Last Century, to an Amazon "Zero" in this one. *Strange*. I am Winston Smith, working for the People's Well Being, trying to have a Brand when what I really have is a brain. And that brain is swimming very, very hard to come up on the other side, open its eyes and breathe.

Perry Brass was born in Savannah, Georgia, and is currently living in New York City. Poet, author, and playwright Perry Brass has published 19 books, including poetry, novels, short fiction, science fiction, plays and bestselling advice books (*How to Survive Your Own Gay Life*, *The Manly Art of Seduction*, *The Manly Pursuit of Desire and Love*). He has been a finalist six times for Lambda Literary Awards, has won five IPPY Awards from the Independent Publishers Group and was a finalist for a prestigious Ferro-Grumley Fiction Award from New York's Ferro-Grumley Foundation. Active in the movement toward lesbian, gay, bisexual, and transgender rights since 1969, Brass' work deals with issues of sexual freedom, spirituality and personal politics coming out of his involvement with the Gay Liberation Front right after the Stonewall Rebellion. He has written about and anticipated in his work much of the progressive change we see today throughout the world—around gay marriage, economic justice, gender equality, reproductive freedom, men's health issues and transgender rights.

He also writes regularly for the *Huffington Post*. For more information: www.perrybrass.com

Goodbye My Safety Blanket
By Stephen B. Pearl

When I first read Gorge Orwell's *1984* I was comforted, oddly enough, by economics. The expense of the massive video surveillance system seemed prohibitive and at that time, the 1970s, it was. Now I look around me and that comfort has evaporated. The sheer scope of our reliance on interactive technologies has made us vulnerable to the kind of technological totalitarianism that Orwell predicted and it has happened and is happening so gradually that most of us remain unaware.

Who hasn't watched a cop show where they pull images from traffic cameras and other sources to track down the bad guy? We, the taxpayers, have embraced this kind of 'security' in the name of law and safety, but how far should it extend? Recently the police in my own city were encouraging homeowners to network their private security cameras into a police—read government—database so that criminals in residential neighborhoods could be more readily tracked. So now not only is Big Brother watching, but he is making you pay for it directly.

An other example of you paying for your own surveillance is the recent news about how smart TV's and computers can feed back data allowing corporations access to the living rooms and studies of much of the world's population. In short, if you have a device hooked up to the Internet in a room, you have forfeited your privacy. Of course the device must be set up to send the type of data down the line that is being monitored. A TV without a camera could be used to monitor conversations through the speakers but would not have visual. Add a camera and you add visual. So keep in mind the next time you and your beloved decide to spice things up with a little pay-per-view that you may not be the only one being entertained.

One interesting aspect of this kind of monitoring is the device has to be powered up; note I didn't say turned on. Most modern TV's DVRs and the like never turn fully off. The manufactures have sold this as a quick start feature or a necessity to keep the internal clock running. Personally, I don't mind waiting a few seconds for my TV to warm up and I question why a battery, similar to those used in computers, couldn't maintain the clock setting and turn on the power at a pre-programmed point. The battery could recharge during device operation. Environmentalists have been cautioning us about these 'phantom loads' for years. Since easy technical solutions exist for this problem, I can only wonder why they haven't been applied. Is there an ulterior motive?

It has been within the realm of technological capability to monitor the sound in a room through the telephone receiver without the use of any other in-house equipment for a couple of decades now.

I am strongly reminded of how in *1984* the protagonist had a TV over-looking his room and the only place that offered any privacy was a closet built behind the TV's line of sight. Only by virtue of the fact that Winston Smith lived in a building built before the TV technology came about was he able to have any privacy at all.

Another aspect of this technological totalitarianism is in our move towards a paperless society. Once a piece of information is committed to paper, or some other enduring medium, it is fixed; it takes a great deal of effort to eradicate it. This is not the case with the electronic medium. Files can be uploaded and downloaded with ease, text altered remotely. Lies are truth and with the subtle manipulation of supporting evidence, false truth can be documented.

I recall a story about Wikipedia from a few years ago where there was a battle over a statement that George Washington owned slaves. Apparently this fact was posted but various proponents of white-washing history kept taking it down. The last time I looked, Wikipedia did include the fact that Washington kept slaves but also said that he spoke against slavery as being contrary to the ideals of the New United States. What this illustrates is that when the supporting evidence can be changed, the perceived 'facts' are also fluid. This was a recurring theme in *1984*

I remember a scene from *1984* where Winston kept a secret paper journal and he had recorded that the chocolate ration had been cut to a certain amount due to setbacks in the war. The following day the announcement was that the chocolate ration had been increased to that same set amount because of successes in the war. The populous cheered the news. Only because Winston had recorded the information in his journal did he know different from the masses.

In my *Tinker* series of books, I write about a dystopian nation state that practices a form of corporate feudalism, the United Grid Regions. One aspect of this nation state is government control of the entertainment broadcasts and media. In *Tinker's Sea,* a United Grid Regions agent speaks about the entertainments that are forbidden from the populous at large. In his nation there is no mention of Robin Hood, Spartacus, The American Revolution and several other tales because they deal with a rebellion. The thought parallels much of Orwell's work in so much as the very notion of rebellion is so de-emphasized that the populous can't even conceptualize it. With centralized control of the media this is a real possibility.

Today the news media is largely controlled by a few major corporations. In short, while it may not be under direct government control, it can be argued that the media is controlled by those who really pull the puppet strings. Secondary media, the Internet, is largely unfiltered and littered with fake, satirical news stories making it an unreliable source of information. If a movement begins in the current era, it has to battle through a flood of news and chatter to be seen and, only if the powers that be decide not to bury it under the latest celebrity scandal, will the story see the light of day. Those avenues that a movement can use to get the message out cannot be trusted because fiction masquerading as fact often erodes credibility. As such, steering the popular consciousness becomes the privilege of an elite few. Once more Orwell made this point clear.

Other means of tracking the herd that are notable are the transponders in vehicles. Credit and interact transactions, if you want to get fancy, satellites in low earth orbit. Cellular phones with GPS, laptops with GPS, low jack systems in cars, and, coming soon, autopay systems where instead of waiting for a teller or a pay station, you just walk out the door and your card, as well as your purchases, are scanned.

One aspect that Mr. Orwell couldn't really have predicted is the vast amount of artificial intelligence that can be brought to bear to pull all these technologies together.

It is a fact that government computers scan emails for key words and flag them as security risks. There was a housewife who sent an email that her child's play had bombed and found herself on a watch list. Being a fiction writer, I have a personal fantasy of a government agent in some secret bunker slipping into the toilet stall with an early version of one of my works 'to assess' the computer's flagging of me as a threat and determine whether or not I warranted further inspection. I hope he enjoyed the read; I'm always open to reviews.

The fact is we now have the computing power to do, at the least, preliminary screening of the mass of data the above methods can bring in. With that, screening patterns can be detected and if the state deems those patterns undesirable, actions can be taken.

Thus, I have had my security blanket ripped away by advancing technology and the clever way the government manipulates us into paying for our own enslavement. The real question we must ask ourselves is how much do we trust our government? Further, how much do we trust our system of government? Big brother is watching and somebody has given him binoculars. I think that Orwell must be spinning in his grave that his cautionary tale has been used as an instruction manual, and that we, the sheep, have so willing traded our privacy to the wolves for the promise of security and convenience.

Stephen B. Pearl is a speculative fiction writer who in his Tinker series of novels addresses a post-apocalyptic world and two budding societies, one potentially utopian and the other dystopian.

He has lived through the rise of technologies that have the potential to free humanity and propel us to the stars or enslave us in the deranged imaginings of some of the lowest of our kind. Being Canadian, Stephen watched the cold war between the Soviet Union and the United States play out and remembers the serious talk with his parents about if his family members became separated but survived the nuclear war, (yea, right) where they were to meet. The broadcasts from that time followed by a little research lead him to believe the enemy shouldn't be a nation state but the manipulative puppet masters that run it. A Russian man wants little more than to provide for the woman who loves him and his children and maybe have a quiet drink in front of the TV after a hard day's work. Sound familiar? It should. We are the same at the core.

George Orwell's *1984* disturbed Stephen deeply as a teen because he saw how we were marching towards the world it warned against. As an adult, Stephen ponders the changes and the obvious manipulations as well as the shear fecklessness of the general populous and it makes him want to weep. For more about Stephen and his works visit: www.stephenpearl.com or Amazon: www.amazon.com/author/stephenpearl

Archie Andrews' Orwellian Adventure
By Tim Hanley

When I was 13 years old, I bought George Orwell's *1984* because I saw it mentioned in an Archie comic book and thought that it could be a fun read.

The Archie story was reprinted in a digest, and was originally published as "It's 1984 at Riverdale" in *Archie at Riverdale High* #95 in February 1984. Written by Rick Margopoulos with art by Stan Goldberg and Rudy Lapick, the tale centered on Mr. Weatherbee, the principal of Riverdale High, going power mad with a new security camera system that had just been installed in the school. He told his students, "From my central control room, I can **watch** any student, **anywhere**, at any**time**!" and ordered them to be on their best behavior. Not only was the new system invasive, it was imperfect. When Betty Cooper stumbled and Archie Andrews caught her, Mr. Weatherbee just saw Betty in Archie's arms and assumed, "**Ah-ha**! Just as I thought... Archie's up to his usual **antics** with the **girls**!" He then threatened them both with detention.

Upset by this constant surveillance, Archie remarked, "I swear, it's turning into *1984* around here," and explained George Orwell's novel to Jughead Jones, Veronica Lodge and the rest of the gang. He told them about Big Brother and the Thought Police, and how "the government spied on all the people, told them what to read—even **brainwashed** them how to **think**!" The gang was gravely concerned, and later saw echoes of Orwell's dystopia elsewhere in Riverdale, including a faulty bank computer system run amok and a government crackdown on the press that sent Reggie Mantle's reporter father to prison.

All of the situations were eventually resolved. Genius Dilton Doiley bested the computer with ease, while the ever-sneaky Reggie Mantle convinced the mayor to free his father with some crafty blackmail. Mr. Weatherbee's downfall was even more comedic. It began when he was monitoring Ms. Beazly, the cafeteria chef, and told her that she should add more salt to her mashed potatoes. She was so offended that she covered the video camera lens with a splat of the mash and quit her job, forcing Mr. Weatherbee to momentarily abandon his surveillance to finish the day's meal himself. When he later returned to his control room, the main panel blew up in his face; he'd purchased the system from "Discount Harry," and the faulty equipment meant that he had to disconnect the entire network lest it burn down the school if it flared up again.

All in all, it was an amusing story. I was the sort of 13 year-old who still got a good laugh out of an Archie comic (little has changed now that I'm in my early 30s), and when I saw *1984* at a bookstore soon after, I decided to pick it up. I was anticipating a sort of adventure tale, a heroic battle against an oppressive government that would be overthrown by the power of the people. I was not expecting the bleak journey of a nebbish office worker whose rebellion was not only quashed but doomed from the second it began. Orwell's *1984* was one of the first "serious" books I ever read and, while it left me somewhat shocked and alarmed, it stuck with me and opened my eyes to the workings of power and control. Subsequent re-readings have only furthered my appreciation of the text and its evergreen applicability.

The novel has been a cultural touchstone since its publication in 1949, constantly referenced and alluded to throughout all forms of media. There is a perpetual relevancy and adaptability to *1984*. In disparate sources ranging from Apple commercials to *30 Rock* to *Doctor Who*, Orwell's concepts and imagery slip into our popular culture frequently and with ease. The book is always pertinent to political matters as well, especially in these days of "alternative facts" and constant moments of Doublethink. While it's perhaps disconcerting that this dystopian text is so often germane in such varied situations, it's also encouraging that we have it and the critiques it offers when we need it. Still, despite its ubiquity, *1984* is certainly an odd inspiration for a children's comic book.

Archie comic books are hardly radical texts. In the issue before "It's 1984 at Riverdale," Archie and the gang recounted their summer vacation adventures. The issue that followed it was essentially an anti-smoking PSA, with all of the drama and gravitas of an after-school special. Archie comics are known for humorous antics and broad moral lessons, and encouraging kids to view both their school administration and the government as oppressive Big Brother figures was an unusual angle, to say the least. It was a big shift from Jughead eating too many hamburgers or Archie's jalopy going on the fritz again.

And yet, it's fitting in a way. The children in *1984* were the Party's biggest supporters and most dedicated informants. They followed Big Brother without question, were the most frenzied viewers of the Two Minutes Hate, and even put Party over family by regularly turning in their parents for being thought criminals. As Orwell wrote, "It was almost normal for people over thirty to be frightened of their own children." The authoritarian system was engrained in children from birth, and they were constantly indoctrinated with its principles everywhere they looked.

Archie comic books perform a similar function, though far less insidiously so. In between all of their amusing hijinks, Archie and the gang serve as exemplars of good citizenship for young readers. There are innumerable lessons about how to be a decent friend and neighbor, the importance of education and obeying your parents, and the values of honesty and integrity. These are all important messages but, as Orwell demonstrates, children often take in lessons blindly, without question. Perhaps Margopoulos, Goldberg, and Lapick were inspired by the novel and crafted a story with a moral that encouraged kids to question authority and not just automatically accept what their teachers, politicians, or even comic books told them.

Unlike me, it's doubtful that many readers rushed out to pick up *1984*, but the story itself mimicked its themes and encouraged questioning of those in power. Even though Riverdale was a far less sinister setting than Oceania, the broad strokes of Orwell's dystopia easily translated into this typically wholesome comic book environment. In doing so, the story captured a key warning inherent in the novel, that despotic control could happen anywhere, and showed that this should be opposed. Whether readers went on to read *1984* or not, then or down the road, because of the adaptability of the text and this subversive tale in the unlikeliest of places, kids were introduced to some of the core concepts of the novel and ideas that could one day expand their worldview.

Nearly 30 years after "It's 1984 in Riverdale," Big Brother recently came up again in another Archie comic book. A reality television show was set to follow the students of Riverdale High at school, at home, and everywhere they went, constantly filming the teens. Ms. Grundy, a teacher at the school, was unimpressed with the loss of privacy this perpetual filming involved and remarked, "Hmph! Talk about **Big Brother**!" before opining about Orwell and *1984*. Maybe this story has inspired a new generation of readers to seek out the novel, or at the very least caught the attention of a few curious young nerds like me.

Tim Hanley is a comic book historian and the author of *Wonder Woman Unbound: The Curious History of the World's Most Famous Heroine*, *Investigating Lois Lane: The Turbulent History of the Daily's Planet's Ace Reporter*, and the upcoming *The Many Lives of Catwoman: The Felonious History of a Feline Fatale.* He lives in Halifax, Nova Scotia.

Big Brother Sam
By Boze Hadleigh

In *1984* Big Brother is everywhere, but is never seen and may not even exist. Big Brother is effective because enough people believe in "him" (how much less effective Big Sister…) and are ready to follow— to *conserve*—tradition and surrender many, or most of, their rights to a misguidedly revered symbol of tough, supposedly protective and scary (to "the enemy," whomever that may be) male power. In short, and in politics as well as religion, Big Brother is the right-wing patriarchy.

"He" still dominates the globe: almost all Third World nations and most of the "modern" ones. Big Brother is always institutionalized, be it through monotheistic religions that employ a male sky god as a mouthpiece for the ruling male minority's dictates or the USA's near-deified yet anti-democratic Electoral "College," which in 2000 and 2016 overruled the citizens' vote.

I say "male minority" because a majority of the world's population is not heterosexual male. Yet Big Brother in all his guises upholds and perpetuates the interests of male heterosexuals, usually to the detriment of females of every sexual and affectional orientation, and of gay males.

1984 creeps closer when enough people let it happen. Too many Americans are distracted from larger, seemingly distant concerns by their comforts, including too much food, gadgets, TV, sports, beer and sex or the prospect of it. History proves that most revolutions are empowered by the have-nots. The more prosperous and materialistic a society, the less apt people are to rise from their comfy seats to go out and demonstrate or march, or even stroll to the computer or writing desk to send an e-mail or letter of protest or make an I-take-strong-exception phone call.

Travel illustrates this more vividly than books. I've visited over 60 countries and seen far more *manifestaciones* in Latin America than Europe. I've seen how Venezuela, one of South America's more stable democracies until the advent of loudmouth "reformer" and media-manipulating big-man Hugo Chavez, occupied its citizens' minds —and continues, post-Chavez—with the lure and acquisition of consumer goods, from chic clothes and the latest techno-toys to a staggering range of Disney products for both genders. Making it easier is the Third World's mindless breeding and overpopulation that produces a younger, less sophisticated citizenry. The average Venezuelan is about ten years younger than the average American (not that Venezuela isn't in the Americas). It's easier to distract kids and young people. Those who've lived longer know more about life, people and unfairness. Teens and young adults don't want democracy as much as they want *things*.

So what's the excuse of the over 40% of

Americans eligible to vote who didn't bother in this last presidential election, who didn't think it crucial enough—or discern enough difference between the candidates!—to go vote or vote by mail? What valuable thing did they do in the 60 or fewer minutes that they saved by not voting? The 2016 voter turnout hit a 20-year low. The less participatory a democracy, the less it is a democracy.

In *1984,* the Party's inner workings go unexplained and virtually unchallenged. Not enough people and not enough of the media were outraged enough to demand transparency from Donald Trump about the taxes he paid, or rather, didn't pay (the rich getting richer…). Follow the rules or you're disqualified. But anything goes when most people don't care. Democracy is too easily taken for granted, until it keeps eroding and eventually is gone.

By "most people" I mean those who didn't vote plus those who opted for the defiant, unrepentant rule-breaking bully who basically wasn't called to account, who got away with it.

All politicians are opportunistic, but talk about a double standard. Every misdeed, real or imagined, of Hillary Clinton earned her censure, opprobrium, even hatred. Trump's towering mountain of misdeeds and bigotry—e.g., mocking and imitating a handicapped man—didn't result in appropriate indignation from a complacent and/or bigoted citizenry. Do you think Adolph Hitler was often challenged, even toward the beginning? Did you know Putin's Russia has made it illegal to criticize his government? How Big Brother can you get? Why hasn't U.S. media publicized that more widely? Why always refer to Putin as president of Russia as if that's on a par with president of the U.S. or France, when in fact he is a dictator?

George Orwell's novel foresaw telescreens in every home, and eventually there were TV screens in every home. Later, computer screens. Screens, including the ubiquitous pocket-sized ones, are now more pervasive than in *1984*. True, people can utilize them in ways undreamt of by Orwell, but national dependence on a media that preserves the status quo —which blandly accepts meanness, bigotry (against most groups), lies and fanaticism as legitimate opposition—is more complete than ever.

The "news" is what is chosen to be presented as such. It's less about enlightenment than drama and holding viewers' attention and upholding ratings. Sound bites are the order of the day and night. Clarification and context are minimal. Growing up during the Vietnam War I heard "Viet Cong" hundreds of times, without explanation. I only knew we were supposed to automatically hate them (the South's communists who allied with the North's and opposed foreign intervention, be it French or later American; never at the time did I hear that in Southeast Asia "the Vietnam War" was and is known as "the war of American aggression").

Big Brother, aka *1984*'s The Party, aka The Establishment, does more of our thinking for us than we imagine. *1984* can trigger recognition of contemporary words that elicit the automatic responses intended by our BB. Religion is a major safeguard, tool and weapon of the few in charge. Ergo, "atheism" is hated by most Americans, with or without knowledge of its meaning. A- means not, as in asexual or asymptomatic. Theism is the belief in a creator god—invariably the male sky god—who intervenes in human events. My friend Robert Clary (*Hogan's Heroes*) survived the Nazi death camps ("concentration camps" is less accurate but sounds less drastic). He asks, "Post-Holocaust, how can any Jew not be atheist?"

Few have heard of deism, the belief in a creator god who doesn't intervene in human events....

In the U.S., more than Europe, "socialism" is often confused with communism and may be a dangerous word if uttered amid the ignorant and belligerent. Angela Lansbury, whose British father was a socialist politician, has said that was a fact and a word she had to hide stateside during the McCarthy era and for some decades after.

1984 was penned by an Englishman. Would an American have written it? The U.S. is fundamentally more conservative; the UK did not initiate a McCarthy-type political witchhunt and blacklisting. (Perhaps amusingly, Karl Marx believed communism would first take root in Great Britain.)

American media too often promotes the equivalent of *1984*'s Doublethink, which is contradictory but required thinking, and Newspeak, designed to obviate disagreement or rebellious thoughts. An example of the former: when a communist regime uses "Democratic" in its official name. Example of the latter: the radical right purposely misrepresenting gay civil rights as "special rights." The media blandly popularized the term as if it were merely another point of view instead of a deliberate distortion. Nobody wants any group to have "special" rights, right? Though that's what heterosexual males have.

When Christian Serbs targeted Muslim Bosnians (I don't advocate for Muslims) in ex-Yugoslavia the media persistently called it "ethnic cleansing." The two groups are physically indistinguishable and slightly differ linguistically. The difference—the motive—was religion, that ancient syndrome of my Big Brother is better than your Big Brother. Why the inaccurate term? A country's majority religion is to be held blameless by its rulers' media, be it in a Christian-dominated country or a Muslim-ruled one (dominance vs. rule is a matter of degree, neither democratic).

Thought Police don't only exist in *1984*. The propaganda of words and (very) organized religion elicits expected reactions and the contradictoriness of Doublethink. How often is anti-Semitism still labeled "racial intolerance" when it has nil to do with race? The term hides that the intolerance is religious. Don't blame "our" religion! How often is a fanatic described as "devout," if belonging to the majority religion?

Orwell warned that technology can be bad or go bad. Look at the Holocaust, which wedded hateful exaggeration of difference and the ploy of misrepresenting a minority to fan the flames of majority discontent and win votes with lethal 20th Century technology. As in *1984* with its supra-nations, the Holocaust wasn't achieved by just the Nazis—it was effected via a large or predominant percentage of citizens in Christian countries aiding the instigators to uncover and send their Jewish cousins (pre-power, Christianity was a Jewish cult) off to the death camps. The Nazis, even all the Germans, could never have done it alone. It took a continent.

Religion is typically what the majority believes and holds over the minority. As Big Brother's primary tool of control and conformity it's so ingrained that most people would be surprised or offended if you pointed out that wherever there is more religion, there is less democracy. Until they are given facts. And even then, for religion tells you what to think, and facts don't signify.

Napoleon said religion was necessary to keep the vast majority of poor people from killing the small minority of rich people. Marx called it the opiate of the people, i.e., work and toil for Big Brother in this life, but pray hard enough and don't get out of line and the next life (if there is one) will make up for this vale of tears.

Back to bad technology. Who would ever have guessed the Big Brother likes of Putin could use it to influence U.S. elections, at the presidential and state levels? On a personal level, how much of electronic technology is panacea, an opiate for so many people. "Honey, I'm in the canned vegetables aisle of the supermarket right now. Should I buy beets or spinach? Never mind, I see the dessert aisle's just one over. Talk with you in five minutes."

Or "I'm in the library now, I can't talk." And then they talk for five minutes. What was the aim of going to the library? Computer games? Watching an old TV show? Porn? Texting while sitting before a computer? Checking out a DVD? Libraries used to be about books and, along with occasional entertainment (chiefly novels), learning. Nor were they the habitual hangouts of the homeless and mentally challenged, often asleep in front of the inevitable screen.

I once read in a book—it occurs to me Ray Bradbury's *Fahrenheit 451* could be deemed the sequel to *1984*—that the most powerful force on earth is inertia. Big Brother counts on it. It keeps him in power. How often do people talk rather than act? Did you ever know one person who liked setting the clocks ahead so that it gets dark earlier? Yet has that ever been put on the ballot? (Unlike whether to give gay people rights, which isn't democracy, it's an abuse of democracy.) Time-changing isn't inevitable or a natural law. Arizona doesn't observe daylight savings time (of course, Arizona didn't observe Martin Luther King Day either).

Likewise the Electoral College ("college" lends a dignity and wisdom it lacks). It's so U.S.-traditional and old that it's revered automatically. Almost anything via the Founding Fathers is venerated, yet the same pioneering male Establishment endorsed slavery—actual, of blacks, and virtual, of women— and enfranchised only white Christian heterosexual (or passing) land-owning males. In practically everything, everyone and everywhere there's good and bad. It serves the common interest not at all to deify or demonize. Reality dwells between the extremes.

But do you believe the Electoral College will ever give way to actual democracy? People may talk....

Additionally, when a country is as massive and self-contained (excepting Made in China!) as the U.S., it's a world unto itself. Many, or most, Americans are unaware of other nations' realities. It's easy to call one's country great and complacently sit back and imagine everyone else lags far behind. But look at international statistics on health, longevity, crime, quality of life, education, etc. Look how much more Americans pay for needed pharmaceutical drugs (not that a huge percentage of prescribed drugs aren't needed) than Europeans or Canadians. If enough people became proactive instead of, say, pro-complaintive, that could change.

But the word "boycott" is almost a historical curiosity, except in rare instances, and how many people have actually practiced that phrase we've heard so often in movies and TV: Write your Congress(man)?

So near and yet so far: Canada. Some two decades back, our nearly ignored neighbor passed the Personal Information Protection and Electronic Documents Act, prohibiting all entities from gathering any personal information on someone without their consent and using it for commercial purposes. Identity theft was decimated. Were such a law enacted here it would eliminate all data warehouses, Internet information brokers and the credit reporting agencies. But don't hold your breath. Our Big Brother doesn't want that. And Americans don't want it enough to empower it.

Amending or expanding one's thinking also comes up against inertia. The Thought Police have trained us to limit our logical behavior. On the Game Show Network I recently saw a man win $25,000 on *SuperPassword* thanks to a male celebrity. The man was understandably thrilled but instead of hugging the male celebrity in thanks—he gave him a handshake— he turned to the nearest female and hugged her as if she'd earned him the money. A hug is not sexual, but fear can be. Big Brother preys on people's fears, especially males. How much of being "a man" consists of what *not* to do, how not to behave? Perhaps manly anxiety is a key factor in men's having shorter lifespans than women—the gender physically beset by menstruation and childbirth. So who's really stronger?

The reality is that the U.S. has long been at the forefront technologically and economically, as it still is in many instances. But not socially. Whether it's abolishing slavery, giving women the vote, enacting gay civil rights including gay marriage, free childcare, universal healthcare, etc., the U.S. has traditionally lagged behind. Despite its self-image. The U.S. has a lower percentage of female politicians than most First World countries. Many nations, including Third World ones, have elected female heads of state. Some have already had two, including New Zealand and Great Britain. When will it happen here? Can it happen here, with an "Electoral College" and an aggregate majority that is either anti-female (Big Brother is more reassuringly familiar) and/or too tired or bored or trivialized to bother with democracy?

Boze Hadleigh is the author of *Hollywood Gays* and *Hollywood Lesbians: From Garbo to Foster* (both published by Riverdale Avenue Books) and 20 other titles. He has an M.S. in mass communications and speaks five languages. His father was a UC history professor.

1984 and The Year of My Dystopia
By Tracy Lawson

I spent seventh grade in a dystopian haze, haunted by thoughts of totalitarian regimes, privations, curtailed personal freedoms, ubiquitous surveillance technology, and nuclear war, Oh, and those awful utilitarian jumpsuits everyone had to wear.

Why, you ask? Well, it was like this…

Back in the '70s, young adult fiction as we know it did not exist. When I was in elementary school, I read the Laura Ingalls Wilder books, and mystery series starring the likes of Nancy Drew and Trixie Belden. I was one step off from reading books about bunnies and rainbows.

But in my junior-high English class, we were assigned *Fahrenheit 451, 1984, Animal Farm, Lord of the Flies, On the Beach, Fail-Safe, Brave New World* and *Flowers for Algernon.* We plowed through the bulk of the classics in the dystopian genre, with a science-fiction chaser and a couple Cold War propaganda novels and their film versions thrown in for good measure. (Thank God they didn't assign *Clockwork Orange* until high school.)

I was a fairly sheltered 12 year-old, and I was

terrified by what I read. I'd never seen a scary movie in my life. I had no frame of reference for the suffering in those books, didn't connect with the characters, and found it hard to imagine societies and worlds so different from my own. I didn't see these books as social commentary, as warnings, or as calls to arms. They were English assignments, and dreaded ones at that.

Years later, I choose to write in the young adult dystopian genre. Because now I get it. I weave exciting stories to entertain my readers and get them to think about what kind of world they'd like to live in. Frankly, writing YA dystopian fiction rocks.

Dystopian novels are combination horror stories and cautionary tales, set against twisted versions of perfect societies. Dystopian heroes are discontented— they don't fit in, and often lack the self-awareness to realize why.

Teens (like the little ol' seventh-grade version of me) who aren't yet ready for the heavy-hitting social commentary in the classics of the genre may find those same themes and messages, presented in the context of a YA book, much more palatable.

In YA dystopian societies, civilization is usually managed by absent adult authority figures. For teenagers who fear they've inherited a chaotic world, yet feel stifled by the rules, these fictional societies resonate. Dystopian societies take rule making to the extreme. Extreme control. Extreme censorship. Extreme surveillance. No dissenting ideas. In these societies, parents and children are often subjected to the same controls and restrictions.

The classic dystopian novel tends to be more apocalyptic, and reveals dire consequences for those who dare to defy the powerful. YA dystopia can be apocalyptic and scary—but it can also feel a lot like high school, where everyone feels pressure to conform. To escape the fear, alienation, and danger, protagonists band together with others like themselves.

YA dystopian fiction opens a pathway to explore and appreciate the genre—and appreciating makes it easier for teens to fully absorb the messages in the classics when they're assigned to read them at school, or choose to read them for pleasure.

When readers meet my protagonists, they realize that Tommy and Careen are teenagers with interests, hopes, and dreams much like their own, who are a threat to society because they rebel against the totalitarian Office of Civilian Safety and Defense. In order to maintain control, the OCSD director has to convince everyone that the threat of terrorism overrides their rights as individuals, and their loss of freedom is a small price to pay for safety. But who is the greater threat? Who is the real cause of terror in their society?

Adolescent leanings toward personal liberty and independent thought are right and worthy. A healthy diet of classics like *1984* and more recent books like my Resistance Series will provide a sobering look at the extremes to which control can be asserted over people who fail to stand up for themselves question authority.

Finally, I write dystopian fiction in the hopes that it will remain fiction. I further hope that some of the students who read my work will one day take up the charge and write their own stories of rebellion, independence, and liberty.

Tracy Lawson is a native of Cincinnati, Ohio, is the author of the award-winning young adult dystopian Resistance Series books. She strives to craft exciting and thought-provoking stories in the hopes that dystopian fiction will remain just that—fiction.

Tracy, a former dance teacher who nowadays choreographs musicals in her spare time, is married with one grown daughter and two spoiled cats. She divides her time between Dallas, Texas and Columbus, Ohio.

Follow Tracy
Twitter: @TracySLawson
Facebook: http://facebook.com/tracylawsonauthor
Resistance Series website:
http://counteractbook.com

1984 and Walden: A Time and A Place in Two Volumes

By Tamara Rose

Early on in *1984*, Winston, the main character, listens to Parsons bragging about his daughter's cleverness. She had been hiking with her troop (think Girl Scouts) and she and her friends break off to follow a strange man through the woods. When they finally emerge, they report the man to the police patrols. Instead of reprimanding the girl for getting separated from her group, or cautioning her against following someone deemed dangerous, the father seems proud of her risk-taking. She had noticed that the man was wearing "a funny kind of shoes," and thus suspected he was a foreigner. And thus probably an enemy agent, and thus possibly worthy of being reported. And the next logical assumption is that he will be shot. That is the world of *1984*.

Henry David Thoreau was a guy who wore funny shoes. He regularly took long walks in the woods, usually four hours a day. In fact, he had wandered back into town from his cabin in the woods by the pond to pick up a pair of repaired shoes on that fateful day when he was put in jail, If it wasn't for a pair of funny broken shoes, *Civil Disobedience* might never have been written. In *1984*, the very act of forging your own trail is criminal; any form of disobedience and independence is quickly killed off. You are only allowed to march to your own drummer if it means tracking down an enemy agent for the state.

Walden, one might argue, is the complementary opposite of *1984*. While Orwell paints a picture of a dystopian future in which everyone's thoughts converge, Thoreau goes in the opposite direction. He reminds us what it means to march to our own drummer, to go off into the woods to live deliberately, to confront the essential facts of nature. He disagrees with the capitalists of Concord, he doesn't buy into materialism. He quits teaching when he is forced to discipline students through violence. Winston succumbs to the threat of violence and lives out the rest of his days in quiet desperation. We must consider both books as we teeter on the fulcrum of the present; these books sit on either end of the seesaw.

Both main characters in the books are diarists, collecting thoughts privately on actual paper, "smooth creamy paper." In the dystopian *1984*, all random bits of paper must disappear down "memory holes." In the cabin alongside Walden, the journal is the one item of value in the entire cabin. It is locked up in the desk drawer, every time Thoreau goes into the woods for a saunter.

Walden was published in 1856, during the rise of America's Industrial Revolution, when nature was beginning to be subsumed and fed into the machine of capitalism. Young farm girls were shipped to textile factories, forests were logged, and even the ice on

Walden was cut and shipped overseas. And so, Thoreau turned his keen eye on all that was disappearing in nature and society. He observed ants, foxes, flowers and trees, keeping such meticulous records that he is often called the father of modern ecology. At the time, his neighbors chastised him for wasting the day watching frogs, instead of being industrious. His records are currently being used as baseline measurements for modern climate change. Because of them, we know that on average, flowers bloom 11 days earlier than in Thoreau's day, due to a warmer climate.

Thoreau as an author (and as his own main character) was careful to record everything that he judged to be significant, even if his neighbors did not. In *1984*, Orwell's main character suffers from a peculiar kind of amnesia, one encouraged by the State, He cannot remember the London of his childhood, or what year it is exactly, or the precise moment of the larger societal change of attitude. The State strips away all history, by erasing evidence and reverse-engineering history. Winston has a vague memory of holding a photograph in his hand which has the definitive proof that the State is manufacturing "AltFacts" ("Alternative Facts"-the Newspeak of 2017). And he releases it down the memory hole. Do we as a society choose to remember or choose to forget? And what version of truth do we treasure, and which do we gloss over, or rewrite?

In fact, let me tell you what Walden (the pond) was like back in 1984 (the year) according to my own memory. I grew up near the pond and learned to swim there. *1984* was on my school summer reading list, and it rode in my beach bag to Walden Pond. In the year 1984, there were no iPhones, like today. There were kids in swimsuits and parents on shore. There were cameras, yes, but they were rare. There was no Walden Pond video game. There was something that no longer exists, a giant cement dock for kids to jump off of, on the Main Beach. A hundred years before that, there was also a railroad stop, that would bring you to an amusement park and a racetrack. That was removed too. In 1984, it was just a beach for families. Some might argue that it existed in a time closer to 1817 than 2017. It was a perfect place to escape to. Thirty-three years later, it is more notable for its rarity as a preserved piece of parkland (how much longer will that last?) and for the fact that there is no cell or Wi-Fi service along the shores. It is known as a technological dead-zone. But everything else in its ecosystem is alive and thriving.

It is we who have changed.

Walden the book, has not changed with the times, yet has aged well. We are the ones who now understand its relevance. It is one of the first true multimedia books we have. The best way to read it is with your feet in the sand. Open to a random page, read until the sun warms you up and you are ready for a swim, or a walk. Go interact with the landscape before you. Come back to shore and open it again. Repeat. Better than a video game.

1984 is a different kind of multimedia thought experiment. The absurd headlines and clickbait reveal deeper truer levels of the book. If history could be subjected to gamification, we would be unlocking the highest levels of achievement. All the absurd political fictions are now coming true, additional points racked up with each revolution of the 24-hour news cycle. Having been published in 1949, it does not predict Google or iPhones exactly, but instead comes up with a series of metaphors that now allow us to fill in the blanks. Other more recent fictions offer storylines closer to the details of the modern world. *The Circle* by Dave Eggers explores Google as the totalitarian regime and makes the information dictate the State. (Author's Note: In case this essay is found in the not-so-distant future, I want to make sure not to offend. A monopoly is not a bad thing, and I, for one, welcome our robot overlords!) *The Man in the High Castle* episodic series helps us to imagine the alternate storyline of history. Even as we are living in one right now.

We used to live in the time of Thoreau and *Walden*, but now in 2017, we live in *1984*. Everyday, the "AltFact" statements get better, by which I mean, more amusing. More improbable. Including, but not limited to, the use of microwave ovens for spying. I wonder how long it will be before we all stop laughing. Or stop crying.

In the present moment, we seek to be individuals, and if we are lucky, smart or rich, perhaps we can reach a level of immortality. For those of you writers who despair that your own most significant writings will forever remain lost or buried in a drawer or in a giant reject pile, take heart. At one point, Thoreau had to take back all the unsold copies of his own book from his publisher, 700 plus volumes. He lived more of his life as a failed writer than a successful one and would be astounded at his level of legend.

Winston is afraid that no matter how many times he writes or doesn't write, or even destroys his thoughts, the Thought Police will get him. His thoughts will be made public, while he himself will be vaporized. He writes anyway.

We live in a moment of history where writing is democratized. This side of the digital divide, everyone can have a voice. Ironically and absurdly, the only limitation of everyone's blog posts, Twitter feeds, Facebook posts and Google history is limited to the power and elegance of the Search. Truth exists and persists, but it cannot always be found. The message of both books is the same, no matter the suffering, the future depends on you recording the truth.

WRITE ANYWAY.

Tamara Rose's short story "Making of a Modern Woman" appears in *The Morris-Jumel Anthology of Fantasy and Paranormal Fiction*. Her Concord series of plays (so far) include *Sense, Thoreau Vs. Schultz* and *Transcendental Ghosts of Fairyland Pond*. She holds an MBA and an MS in Human Factors in Information Design, and works as a proud steampunk Woman in Tech.

What We Desire Must Be Valued
By Rona Gofstein

I could not survive in the world of George Orwell's *1984*. All that I most value, support and am inspired to write about is lacking in that dystopian creation, and when I see that happening in any way in our world today, I speak out.

I deeply believe that being able to pursue your dreams, your heart's desire, makes life worth living, No matter what those dreams—big, small, personal or world-changing—we should be free to go for what motivates us, what inspires us. The most amazing things in our world have happened because someone was "crazy" enough to try and others were crazy enough to support him or her. I think that is wonderful.

Knowing what I want and working towards it has guided almost all the major decisions of my life from where I went to college, to starting my career as a writer and even my choice of a partner. I could not have married a man who did not support, encourage and believe in me. As a parent, it is at the heart of what I want for my children; my older son works daily toward his goal of playing professional sports while building his own business, and I make certain he has what he needs to do this. My younger son has been saying since he was eight that he wants to be a movie director. Six years later he is still committed to this dream, and I am committed to supporting what he needs to learn and do to achieve this. The relationships in my life are vital and loving.

As for me? I write romance, something that becomes twisted and reviled during the course of the novel. For Winston Smith, the main character of the novel, love and hope and the power of relationships are manipulated for the will of the government. He is shown how wrong he is, how stupid and misguided he has become because of what is made to happen during the course of his relationship with Julia. He has his soul broken by O'Brien, the friend to whom he thought he could reveal his true self.

In my novels, and my life, the opposite is true, Not only do my characters have their own goals and dreams, but with the attention and love of a strong partner they are more capable than ever of achieving them.

We deserve relationships that support us.

We deserve the freedom to pursue our dreams.

And yet the threat of the totalitarian world of George Orwell's *1984* is clearly visible today. The power of an omnipresent Internet combined with fears of terrorism have led to a rise in Big Brother-like activity in our country and elsewhere. Every time people are willing to give up liberty for a perceived increase in safety, we lose more of our autonomy and give those who deal in fear the power they crave. Thought Police and "Thoughtcrime," two things I believe we are dangerously close to accepting, cannot be allowed to exist.

We need a world, and our children deserve a world, where we have the freedom, the support and encouragement to go for our dreams, to try crazy things, to imagine a place of greater innovation and achievement. The thought of a world without that liberty? Where my choices and those of my children are limited, watched, curbed and dictated? That world, that country, is no place I would want to live.

Rona Gofstein believes in inspiring others to learn and live their hearts' desires. Her passions include her family, friends and anything to do with shopping, coffee and chocolate. Writing as Rachel Kenley, she is the author of five romance novels and many short stories and blogs on her website www.rachelkenley.net

George Orwell Through the Looking Glass
By Melli Pini, M.A.

1984 is the definitive dystopian novel setting the stage with the now all-too familiar, ominous future of surveillance, mind control and Big Brother dominating society. Headed by the elite Inner Party in the super-state of Oceania, the omnipresent and ambiguous Big Brother is the party leader for whom all reverence, and rebellion, exists. In the face of deliverance from independent thought and free will, Winston Smith is the "last man in Europe" (Orwell's original title for the book), whose innate curiosity and intellect drive him to seek liberation from the control of the Inner Party. Many details of the 1949 plot resonate with the social and political power structures of today's 2017, from the Ministry of Truth (controlled media) to the Thought-Police (NSA), to Ingsoc (socialism/communism) and the distinctions in social classes.

These issues, however, have been present throughout humanity's history. The political climate of World War II and its associated political ideologies such as socialism, nationalism and fascism chillingly echo the era in which this book was written. This is a brave new world of totalitarianism, in which we lose our most precious rights to freedom of thought, and these social realities guide the narrative while teasing the darker underbelly of possibility.

In 2017, in the overt glare of an increasingly dystopian popular media culture (no one can miss the irony of the reality TV shows, even one entitled "Big Brother"), much of George Orwell's predictive *1984* has indeed emerged as the subtext of our 21st Century lives, though not in the way we imagined!

With the recent Trump inauguration and shifts in our political climate, Orwell's Big Brother, despite appearances, is in fact our dystopia's second cousin once-removed; the antiquated elephant in the room. It is our own desire to expose and display ourselves to each other through the power of universal technology that codifies, and ultimately restricts our freedom. These advances in technology were unimagined by Orwell.

We are experiencing a silent collective suicide through willful activity. We happily jump, leap, and plummet to the death of our own autonomy. Voyeurism has become the pulse of voluntary-information-sharing, feeding a larger epidemic of data collection. Moreover, resistance to freedom of thought is masked because of our own participation in, and creation of, this technological "Big Brother." We are engaging in the greatest conformity and self-censorship, and surrendering the privacy of our own selves under the guise of "freedom of thought," when we share opinions, selfies, private photos, videos, favorite foods and purchases. Every second of our cumulative lives is being dumped into an info-vat of uncontrolled permanence. Is this our free will at work?

Or is our self-exposing compulsion becoming an arm of an invisible technological system-at-large? Who or what can we blame for this?

As the lines between identity and data blur, a new kind of human has emerged on the prolific and myriad social platforms birthed by technology. We tend to neglect the fact that technology is literally changing our brains: As Nicolas Carr stated in his 2008 *Atlantic* article on Google and stupidity, "the media or other technologies we use in learning and practicing the craft of reading play an important part in shaping the neural circuits inside our brains." As technology amasses knowledge, experience, power and history into a repository of its own dictatorship, *this* is our new political party.

How does *1984*'s ominous prediction reconcile 2017's reality? *1984* disconnects with 2017 at the point of technology. While technology plays an integral role in the concept of surveillance, in the novel the *telescreen* serves merely as a prop, an instrument of human control. Though "Big Brother" accurately plays out the panopticon of our imprisonment: a prison in which we are constantly observed, with its attendant behavior correction, discipline and punishment, this widescreen character barely mimics today's technology. Thus, the narrative only reflects the psychology of human control. Limited to binary concepts we are all too familiar with: power, dictatorship, totalitarianism, *1984* falls by the wayside of historical analysis.

As French philosopher and social-political theorist Michel Foucault wrote in *The History of Sexuality, Volume I,* "Where there is power, there is resistance, and yet, or rather consequently, this resistance is never in a position of exteriority in relation to power ... there is no single locus of great Refusal, no soul of revolt, or pure law of the revolutionary." Here Foucault shines light upon a flaw in Orwell's vision of dystopia. Foucault's "power" can actually never fully be possessed by one individual, institution or governing body. Thus Orwell misses the mark: in today's world it is our collective participation in technology that ultimately defines and controls us.

But, how could one have even fathomed this world nearly 70 years ago, when we ourselves are grappling to understand it today? Mind control was at the forefront of Nazism, but technology not so much. However, just three days after *1984's* publication, on June 11, 1949, Alan Turing, the father of computer science, postulated in *The London Times*, "I do not see why [the machine] should not enter any one of the fields normally covered by the human intellect, and eventually compete on equal terms." So ahead of his times, yet, I wonder if he had even begun to comprehend how deeply imbedded the circuitry of today's technology would conjoin with the circuitry of our neurobiology.

In all of 2017's technological progress, perhaps we can reimagine Orwell's Inner Party enlisting the likes of Larry Page, Sergey Brin, Mark Zuckerberg and Steve Jobs. Mind control has become the free-reign landscape we call the Internet, the cloud and other variations of our invisible, yet frighteningly real creation. From hackers to the NSA, computer programmers, coders and even middle school-aged smartphone juvenile delinquents, these manifestations of Orwell's historical revisionists are re-scripting our freedom, all in the name of "creativity," "protection" and "advancement."

In 1977, Foucault wrote, "Knowledge, linked to power, not only assumes the authority of 'the truth,' but has the power to make itself true. All knowledge, once applied in the real world, has effects, and in that sense at least, 'becomes true.'"

Rewriting the narrative of our technology-based lives, today's "whistleblowers" Edward Snowden or Julian Assange embody and continue the heroism of Orwell's beloved protagonist Winston Smith. Transparency and truth, transference of knowledge, those are the games only privileged insiders can play. But when will the Big Brother machine take over even its originators, the two percent elite?

What has consumed our desire to observe and participate is now controlling the neural synapses. Compulsive checking rewires our need to check again, and again, and post, and "share," and "share" again. Hardwired to the beat of the same ringtones, graphics and interfaces, are we being primed for homogeny and machinery? When will the rapidfire excess of over-sharing and technology brainwashing destroy us?

Orwell was not too far off from 2017 in his idea of self-imprisonment and mind control. Yet he writes within the framework of our humanity, beautifully preserved in its entire primitive, vulnerable, instinctual and innate desire to compete, take over, devour and oppress our neighbor. The full human *is* the essence of possibility, still retained in Orwell's dark fantasy. Our reality, Orwell's *1984* through a looking glass, presents a far more terrifying present, detrimental, looming and ominous. And this future, at the very moment, is being nurtured and coddled in our very laps, arms, beds, pockets, hands and lives. It is a tsunami of man-made "machinery" that may be drowning the very essence of "us," engulfed in the undertow of our own free will.

Melli Pini earned a B.A. in philosophy from SUNY Purchase and a Masters in Developmental Psychology with a concentration in Creativity and Cognition from Columbia University's Teachers College. She lives on the Upper East Side of Manhattan where she works as global partnerships manager for an executive recruitment and leadership association in Midtown. Aside from having ghostwritten several blogs, PR and marketing pieces, this will be Melli's first publication. Additionally, she can be seen and heard playing live cover music (guitar and vocals) in the occasional bar or restaurant of the NYC grid.

Why Don't You "Like" Me?
By Maximilian Ximenez

The philosopher Jeremy Bentham, in a time when the phrase "jackboot" brought to mind cavalry rather than goose-stepping, proposed the weaponization of human paranoia as a force for social good. A *panopticon*, Bentham proposed, would be a prison designed so that prisoners would assume they were being watched at all times, and that would curb their so-called anti-social behavior, regardless of the fact that the eyes of the prison watchmen might or might not be upon them.

To draw a comparison between Bentham's arguably well-intentioned and Utopian proposal in the 19th Century and George Orwell's terrifyingly omniscient *1984* by way of its telescreens is both trivial and old hat. Far better writers than I have waxed subversive about Orwell's prediction of mass surveillance as a tool of oppression becoming chillingly real, but to date none captures the logical end-point of such a concept: that in the 21st Century, we no longer need to be watched at all to be observed.

I am loathe to admit that I am effusively Millennial, a "digital native" of the "me generation" who has laid his entire life bare to a string of networks.

From the moment I could write I was shooting off my two cents to strangers, leaving a steaming hot trail of information and metrics across newsgroups and chat rooms, pumping social networks with my youthful opinions full of piss and vinegar. I have spent my life not only being observed — I'd be an imbecile to imagine privacy in a post-Patriot Act society — but performing for the camera (why would readers of the Internet want to know my opinions unless they could observe them with their own two eyes?). True, my Internet samizdat did not imperil the state, and the black helicopters did not swoop down upon me because I dared to express my enthusiasm for a particular Spice Girl or season of *Star Trek*. I willingly, if not naively, presented all of this and more to anyone who could decipher my screed, stuck in a lifelong Pavlovian feedback loop seeking reaction, rebuke or reaffirmation for my opinions, totally blind to the true implications of these self-revelations.

To understand the evolution of surveillance in the 21st Century, another great thinker must be elevated to the observant heights of Orwell and Bentham: Zuckerberg. Creator of the preeminent social network, Facebook (which I can only hope may someday be spoken of in much the same way one might mention GeoCities today), Mark Zuckerberg's contribution to the modern panopticon goes beyond what can be seen on the virtual page to what can be inferred with the data.

Some who are my seniors may not interface with Facebook, and those who take pains to protect what shreds of anonymity they can knit together may pride themselves on never using it, but in this day and age that simply is not protection enough. In the 21st Century, not using their service, proverbially hiding from the telescreen, is laughably futile. Everything you've ever said, and more importantly, everything that has ever been said about you by anyone tangentially related to you, has been scooped up by an algorithm to fill out a so-called "shadow profile." Even avoiding the siren call of the social network's comforting "prolefeed" is not enough. You can be tainted by the loosest of associations with undesirables, or the briefest of appearances in the act of impropriety. Such information may not be enough to land you behind bars or whisked away to a CIA blacksite or FEMA death camp quite yet, but my generation has already learned how it can damage our employment, educational and economic opportunities, leading to an exodus away from such sites in ignorance of the telemetry they will continue to track. We will continue to willingly give up our information for entertainment or convenience purposes, or out of simple forgetfulness. Predictably, my generation has refused to act beyond that personal, futile attempt at self-protection.

People my age, and all who have come after me, have learned just how dangerous putting too much information onto the internet can be. When I was a child, of course, the biggest concern was "stranger danger," but now we have to worry about what we say, how we look, what communities we're part of; colleges, employers and potential romantic partners all scroll through our digitized tapestries to find out every bit of information they can. And that, chillingly, is just what has been put up willingly. Appearing in a photograph of a friend who's a felon, using an online forum conflated with degeneracy, all of this is available to anyone with time, determination and a casual knowledge of how to use search engines.

Recent government leaks like the CIA "Vault 7" revelations, or Edward Snowden's disclosure of NSA spying a few years ago, bring us back to Orwell's, and Bentham's, world. What you share, what your friends share and, most chillingly, what AIs and algorithms can put together from what you have **not** shared is available to corporations and the government alike. The modern day panopticon has not just invaded our privacy, but completely obliterated it, and we as a society invited it to do so.

Maximilian Ximenez is a writer, literary agent and self-described "cyberpunk" who graduated from Stony Brook University in 2014 with a degree in English Literature. He currently lives in New York with his two cats and a crushing sense of existential terror. In an uncanny act of self-immolation, he can be found on Twitter at @maxximenez.

2017 Should Not be *1984*
By Sherri Donovan

When I think of *1984,* totalitarian styles of governance come to mind. These are societies where independent thought, diversity and creativity are repressed in the name of maintaining "law and order." The classifying of entire groups of people as the "other" is used to divide, conquer and to squash unity and movement for social change. These societies protect the rich, big businesses, the powerful and the privileged at the expense of the rest of the community, particularly the most vulnerable. We see this in Orwell's *1984* and in the USA today.

Today, increases in funding for police, the military and surveillance have become the norm while economic programs to help the poor, working and middle class have been cut, not to mention slashes to health care, Medicare, public schools and even breakfast programs for children. Simultaneously refusing to let in war refugees and attempting to build a wall along the Mexican border could have appeared in the pages of *1984.*

Fear, prejudice and intimidation are purposely utilized to control and exclude. The recent raids by immigration officials to round up, detain, cage and deport people of color who have been living, working, paying taxes and raising children in the USA smacks of fascistic tactics. Many children have been left without their parents and young, educated students and adults who have been detained or deported have had their dreams shattered. Of course, those who are outspoken about the actions of ICE have been immediately taken.

African-Americans in the USA have always lived in a version of *1984* from slavery to segregation to mass incarceration. Entire industries and private contracts for prisons feed on filling jail cells, where punishment and harassment is the norm. The use of random searches, police brutality, prosecutors' control of grand juries, discriminatory use of draconian drug laws, harsh sentences, solitary confinement and the death penalty have ensured the criminalization and virtual genocide of young black men and, increasingly, black females.

As civil rights attorney Michelle Alexander pointed out in her book *The New Jim Crow*, once one is labeled a felon, a person cannot vote, receive governmental assistance and faces job discrimination.

You are the "other," an Orwellian undesirable and outcast.

Since Trump's presidential campaign and election, hate crimes and threats against LGBT people, Jews, Muslims and other minority groups have increased. Women's rights are also on the radar to be chopped. Trump has vowed to select Supreme Court judges to overturn *Roe v. Wade*, dismantle the right to choose and control our own bodies. The KKK and neo-Nazi groups have been more vocal and active. The gun lobby is golden. Environmental protection, workers and consumer rights are severely challenged.

During this same period, free speech by newspapers and protesters of Trump's policies have been under attack. Dissenters have been arrested and fined. Journalists have been excluded from press conferences and events, even the most mainstream media like CNN and the *New York Times*. States are proposing and passing legislation to stifle demonstrations. Any celebrity like Meryl Streep or politician like Senator Corey Booker who speaks out against Trump is immediately criticized or threatened.

As the recent *New York Times* article, entitled "What Biracial People Know" pointed out, a successful, creative, prosperous, healthy and peaceful nation flourishes on diversity and independent thought. 2017 should not be *1984*. Sadly and alarmingly it is, if we don't resist.

Sherri Donovan is a family attorney and author. She has published nonfiction and poetry books, essays, articles and blogs. Her work has appeared in *The Huffington Post* and *The New York Law Journal*. Her most recent book is *Matryoshka Rising Poetic Briefs* available on Amazon. Sherri is also the founder of Art Helping Life, Inc., a nonprofit that assists impoverished children globally. Sherridonovan.com

Orwell's *1984:* Are We There Yet?
By Sean Fitzpatrick

The second most terrifying thing about George Orwell's *1984* is the supposition that it is possible to destroy humanity without destroying humankind. The first is how many aspects of our democratic nation resemble his dystopian nightmare.

George Orwell wrote *1984* in 1948 as a political satire of a totalitarian state and a denunciation of Stalinism. Orwell himself was a socialist, who fought for the republicans in the Spanish Civil War and was wounded by a sniper bullet to the throat. As the West became aware of the horrors of Stalin, Orwell became disillusioned.

1984 was Orwell's resulting futuristic-cautionary tale of Winston Smith in a world of government domination defined by anxiety, hatred, and cruelty. The Party, whose head is reverently called Big Brother, presides over existence through omnipresent surveillance and mind control. Their subjugated citizens are programmed not only to accept if Big Brother says that $2 + 2 = 5$, but also to believe it. Winston's adventures begin as he slowly and fearfully steps out of the established traces, sensing the hypocrisy that surrounds and penetrates him, to search for truth. What he finds is pain.

Commenting on *1984*, Orwell wrote, "I do not believe that the kind of society I describe necessarily *will* arrive, but I believe that something resembling it *could* arrive."

Has it?

Of course, the United States is not autocratic; but many of the disturbing elements of *1984* actually exist in American society. In some cases, what is happening in the U.S. is more draconian and invasive than anything Orwell conceived.

War is Peace

One of the Party pillars in *1984* is endless war on a global scale. The war, however, is a fabrication accepted and treated as fact. For, unreal as it is, it is not meaningless. World powers become enemies and allies interchangeably simply to keep the masses in perpetual fear, perpetual industry, and perpetual order. War provides outlet for unwanted emotions such as hate, patriotism, and discontent, keeping the structure of society intact and productive without raising the standard of living.

Where is the enemy—or the end—in our "war on terror?" The faceless foe and limitless objectives are productive of a widespread atmosphere of paranoia and restricted civilian liberties. In the wake of the sequestration military-spending cuts, it is also manifest that, to many, war means little more than a job.

Freedom is Slavery'

The perpetual warfare in *1984* sacrifices individual freedom for collective freedom. By submitting entirely to the Party, people surrender their identity and the impulses that arise from having one, passively receiving everything. The principles of *un*freedom and inequality are consciously perpetuated to stifle revolution and uprising, uniting all in a trance under the watchful eye of Big Brother.

True freedom is the unimpeded capacity to realize the human good. Freedom in America is generally defined as mere license, which enslaves when human inclinations stray from the good. This American fallacy defines liberty as getting what is wanted, and moreover, that the government is there to give it. Subservience through mindless entitlement for government handouts and bailouts is not freedom, but slavery.

Ignorance is Strength

Any transgression against the Party is a capital crime. The common habit, therefore, is invincible ignorance: the appearance of orthodoxy without knowing what orthodoxy entails. The Party's world-view is impressed most successfully on people incapable of understanding it.

Has *anyone* read the Affordable Care Act? The plan appears to be to swallow it in blind lip service to the ideologies of big government. This mentality is rendered common by a declining—if not fallen—education system. (Who can afford college anyway these days?) Rather than address the plague of ignorance, America seems more concerned with protecting the ignorant from profiling and unequal opportunity.

Telescreens

Practically every public and private place in Orwell's fictional world is under surveillance through "telescreens" that also broadcast announcements, news and propaganda. They are the sleepless eyes monitoring every move, every word, every facial expression and every involuntary reaction of every person in the effort to detect Thought crime. "Big Brother is watching you."

Social media keeps close record of our "likes" and activities. Our telephone calls and browsing histories are accessible to apparently any NSA analyst, according to Mr. Snowden. Our social security numbers and zip codes are increasingly part of everyday transactions. Private lives are spied upon. Drones fly overhead. Cameras record invisibly. Data is collected. We, too, are being watched.

Doublethink

Party members in *1984* practice a mental contortion that assumes two contradictory premises simultaneously for the sake of exercising control over reality. This practice is called "Doublethink," and leaves no impression that reality has been violated. This mind control, or memory control, allows the Party to shape their world: "Who controls the past controls the future; who controls the present controls the past."

Politicians often use forms of Doublethink when they carefully and consciously lie. National Intelligence Director James Clapper, for instance, was asked at a Senate hearing last March whether the NSA collected information on millions of Americans. "No," Clapper answered. "Not wittingly." Following the NSA leak, Clapper insisted he did not lie, but responded in the "least untruthful manner." We are too accustomed to mutable "truth"—the gospel according to Wikipedia. From conflicting Benghazi reports to misleading Trayvon photographs, the media regularly and unabashedly fabricates, falsifies, and manipulates according to the agenda *du jour*.

Newspeak

A prominent feature of progress in *1984* is the language "Newspeak," a stripped-down, impotent distortion of English. Orwell draws a connection between the success of the tyrannical government and the deterioration of language, as Newspeak renders certain ideas literally unthinkable through reduction of vocabulary and grammar. Language control results in thought control.

We have our own variations of "Newspeak" that limits what we think by limiting what we say. "Politically correct" language is speech that hedges thought. Technological autocorrect and autocomplete functions often dictate our phraseology. Emails and tweets promote stilted communication. And let us not forget text talk, which AFAICT, is not helping anything. WYSIWYG. As a language deteriorates, the grand and noble ideas it is capable of expressing are in danger of deteriorating also.

Although we are not citizens of Orwell's world, there is complacency in our civilization that is akin to Orwellian capitulation. The fears and confusions of a rapidly changing culture and its permeating devices are disorienting and discouraging. Affairs may not be as grisly as they were for Winston Smith, but we may not be far off. After all, can Facecrime really be much different than hate-crime? Is it better for sex to be reduced to its practical purpose or its pleasure? Whether memory holes or paper shredders, a society resembling Orwell's description may have arrived.

There is only so much we can do. When all are monitored, all are suspect.

"We are the dead. Our only true life is in the future. We shall take part in it as handfuls of dust and splinters of bone. But how far away that future may be, there is no knowing. It might be a thousand years. At present nothing is possible except to extend the area of sanity little by little."

Sean Fitzpatrick is a graduate of Thomas Aquinas College and is the Headmaster of Gregory the Great Academy, a boys' boarding school in the Catholic, classical tradition in Northeast Pennsylvania. Mr. Fitzpatrick teaches courses in the Romance and mythology. His writings on education, literature, and Catholic culture have appeared in *Crisis Magazine, Catholic Exchange, The Imaginative Conservative* and *Gilbert Magazine*. He lives in Scranton, PA, with his wife, Sophie, and their five children.

Teaching After Trump
By Melissa Febos

On 9 November, my first thought upon waking was, 'I can't.' I couldn't bear to listen to the stuttering attempts of newscasters making digestible our new terrifying reality. I couldn't bear to hear our president elect's voice piping through the tinny speaker of my radio alarm clock. I couldn't get out of bed. But most of all, I couldn't face my students. Nonetheless, in a few short hours, I was supposed to be at the front of a college classroom in New Jersey.

The day before, I had taught a literature class to 25 students, few of them English majors. I had planned a discussion of the Narrative of the Life of Frederick Douglass, an American Slave. As usual, we opened class with a couple of student presentations on the text.

In my class of 25, there are five obvious students of color, three of them young black women. One of them gave the first presentation. A quieter student, she passed around her handout and stood at the front of the classroom. In a trembling voice, she faced the room full of her white classmates and began to explain race as a social construction. She stumbled and searched for her words. She clenched the piece of paper in her

126

hand, with its bulleted notes. The topic of her presentation was the 'ethical content' of the assigned text, and in this halting manner, but with her head held high, she discussed the 'ethics' of slavery. Just after she described the way slave women had their newborn infants taken from them and sold to other plantations, she paused and stared out at the silent class. She blinked. Just imagine, she said. And then continued.

I don't think the other students saw the tears in my eyes as she spoke, but they heard me clap for a long time after she finished. I wanted to carry her out of that classroom on my shoulders. But I knew there was no place to carry her. As I clapped, I offered a silent, fervent prayer that this election's result would be a step toward a world in which she was safe.

* * *

I live in Brooklyn's Bed-Stuy neighborhood, where my voting location had been 95% full of African-American voters, and the mood on Tuesday morning was warm, even convivial—it was safe to assume we were all there to vote for the same person, and shared a relative confidence in the outcome.

I work, however, in a red county in New Jersey, at a private university where Trump was elected by a small margin in our undergraduate student body's straw poll. Our students are more than 60 % white, with a high number of first generation college students. Despite it being an hour's drive away, many of them have never been to Manhattan. Most of them have never left the country, and some not even the county—for lack of motivation rather than resources. I often struggle to relate to them academically—I was an intellectually ambitious, highly politicized college student who idealized radical feminist thinkers and wrote a senior thesis twice the recommended page length.

I suspect that my students are a pretty ordinary sample of their generation. They are also, on the whole, kind, good-natured and teachable. Some are incredibly talented. In my four years of teaching them, I have calibrated my curriculum to try to reach them, and a lot of the time it does. This requires a kind of creativity I didn't have to employ prior to working there, and is rewarding in ways that I didn't experience teaching other, more cosmopolitan student bodies.

I teach them about feminism without ever uttering the word feminism, because I know how instantly it will alienate my students. I teach intersectionality without ever defining it. I fill my syllabi with women and writers of color, and don't announce it.

My students don't seem to notice. But they read the books. And when I see that flicker of awakening in their faces as they discuss James Baldwin or Jesmyn Ward or Junot Diaz or Joy Harjo and connect their own sympathies with people different from them, sometimes for the first time, I am grateful that I teach here, and not at a school where all of the undergraduates are already fluent in words like hegemony, diaspora, paradigm and intersectionality.

But teaching them requires energy and patience. It requires optimism, a belief that sparking the curiosity or consciousness of a few people every semester is worth it.

Most of the time I am blessed with that optimism. But not on the morning of 9 November.

Like many of us, I went to sleep after the results had turned, but before the winner was officially announced. I desperately wanted to wake up to a different result. I have not felt that kind of pain and fear for my country, for my beloveds, since 9/11. This hurt in a different place—created a chaos inside of me that wasn't mirrored this time in the streets of my city. It changed the way I felt among my fellow citizens, about whom I felt I'd made naive assumptions, even in my relative cynicism.

* * *

Since childhood, my grief has had a refrain: I want to go home.

I grew up in a loving home. My mother was, and still is, a Buddhist psychotherapist and staunch feminist. My father is a Puerto Rican sea captain. They are both Democrats and are both from working class towns in New Jersey much like the one where I teach. I spent my early life carrying signs in peaceful marches and reading while my mother attended meetings of our local National Organization for Women chapter. I also spent a lot of my childhood waiting for my father to return from sea.

I want to go home, I whispered alone in my bedroom at eight years old, missing him. I want to go home, I whispered, alone in my bedroom at 12 years old, after fighting with a class of fellow sixth graders about my right to love another woman. I want to go home, I whispered, alone in my bedroom at 14, after a senior boy grabbed my breast in the high school hallway, meeting my eyes defiantly as he stared down at me. I want to go home, I whispered alone in my bedroom at 20 years old, after shooting speedballs, terrified of the day that my family would find out by way of my own dead body. I want to go home, I whispered alone in my bedroom at 36 years old, on the morning that Donald Trump became our president-elect.

The home that I longed for at eight years old, at 12 and 15 and 20 and 36, was not a literal place. It was a feeling. It was a faith that I, and the people I loved, would be safe. That whatever pain we suffered would pass without killing us, or the parts of us we needed to survive, to thrive, to create love and art and social change.

No matter what our age, this kind of despair manifests in the same way: as a wish that someone will rescue us. A parent, God, a place inside ourselves where we can find refuge and reassurance that everything will be okay.

* * *

I considered canceling my classes. How could I face my students? Ten years ago, when I began teaching, I trained myself to hide my politics. For the first five years of teaching, I even hid my tattoos. Not out of shame, but out of protection. And because I wanted to do my job effectively. I wanted to teach students who had different beliefs than me to love literature, to believe in the inherent value and power of art. To understand how much of our history is archived there. I wanted to turn them into bibliophiles, champions of human rights, believers in their power as compassionate citizens. And most of the time I knew my best chance of succeeding meant hiding how desperately I wanted to succeed.

But Professor Febos did not feel like someone I could be that day. I could only be this devastated woman who wanted to go home. This queer woman sunk in terror for her country. For her loved ones. For all black and brown and immigrant and queer and trans and disabled and female people. For all the boy children, white children, and girls in her country who would learn how to be men, or white, or women—how to be Americans under Donald Trump's administration.

And then, like so many times before, I remembered the person who had always rescued me. The person within me who had built her entire life around the ways she could best keep herself and her loved ones and her country safe. The person who had become a teacher and a writer for precisely those reasons. Because in a country whose government we do not trust, who do we need more than writers and teachers? And what is more powerful than an inspired youth? I turned off the radio. The newscasters would not make it okay. My parents would not make it okay. My students were probably our best hope. And I could reach them faster than anyone.

* * *

Two hours later, as Hillary Clinton gave her concession speech, I walked into my classroom and told my students to take out their notebooks. I had no idea what I was going to say to them. My heart pounded as I stared at their expectant faces. Out of the

15 students in my Introduction to Creative Writing seminar, 12 are young white women, and the other two are young men of color. I have no idea their politics, though I would wager at least a couple of them voted for Trump. I had no desire to alienate any of them. As they dug into their backpacks and produced their pens, I stared at them. I scoured my insides for some trust that underneath whatever differences, we all harbored an earnest desire for the safety and freedom of other humans. To my relief, I found it, a warm ember in my gut that glowed when I touched it.

I told my students to describe a person opposite them in the most obvious ways: race, religion, sexual orientation, country of origin. When their pens slowed, I asked them to describe the country they wish for that person. After a few more minutes, I asked them to think of a child they loved—their own, a niece or nephew, an infant version of themselves. I asked them to describe the country they wished that child to come of age in.

I watched them as they wrote—their smooth foreheads crimped with concentration, their hands moving across notebook pages. When they looked up, I asked them to reconcile those visions into a single vision of a country where both of those realities could exist, and both people would be free to inhabit them. They stared at me for a few beats, and then began writing. Some of them paused, pens hovering over paper as they stared into space and worked out some detail in their minds. They wrote for a long time. When the scratching of pens quieted, I took a deep breath. Something had shifted in the room. We all felt it. As if there was an ember in each of them, stoked by their pens, that had glowed warm and bright enough for us all to see.

I want, I said, searching for my next move. I want you to make a list. They laughed, first quietly, then louder, because this was how I started so many of their in-class exercises, and because they needed so badly to laugh. I want you to make a list of all the things you can do to build this home for us. This time, many of them nodded. They understood what I was asking them to do.

Melissa Febos is the author of the critically acclaimed memoir, *Whip Smart* (St. Martin's Press 2010) and the forthcoming essay collection, *Abandon Me* (Bloomsbury 2017). Her work has been widely anthologized and appears in publications including *Tin House, Granta, The Kenyon Review, Prairie Schooner, Glamour, Guernica, Post Road, Salon, The New York Times, Hunger Mountain, Portland Review, Dissent, The Chronicle of Higher Education Review, Bitch Magazine, Poets & Writers, The Rumpus, Drunken Boat,* and *Goodbye to All That: Writers on Loving and Leaving New York.*

She has been featured on NPR's Fresh Air, CNN, Anderson Cooper Live, and elsewhere. Her essays have twice received special mention from the Best American Essays anthology and have won prizes from Prairie Schooner, Story Quarterly, and The Center for Women Writers. She is the recipient of fellowships from the Bread Loaf Writer's Conference, Virginia Center for Creative Arts, Vermont Studio Center, The Barbara Deming Memorial Fund, Lower Manhattan Cultural Council, and The MacDowell Colony.

The recipient of an MFA from Sarah Lawrence College, she is currently Assistant Professor of Creative Writing at Monmouth University and MFA faculty at the Institute of American Indian Arts (IAIA). She serves on the Board of Directors of VIDA: Women in Literary Arts, the PEN America Membership Committee, and co-curated the Manhattan reading and music series, Mixer, for nine years. She curates literary events, teaches workshops, and speaks widely. The daughter of a sea captain and a psychotherapist, she was raised on Cape Cod and lives in Brooklyn.

Why We Teach *1984* Today
By Ruth-Terry-Walden

When one is a teacher at some point you realize that you are shaping what seminal educator and MacArthur Fellow Lisa Delpit refers to as "Other People's Children" in your classroom each day and each year, thus the choice of what to teach them becomes crucial. There are two texts that our department has placed firmly in its English/Language Arts canon year in and year out and both are dystopian novels that deal with protagonists of different genders yet each are damned for holding fast to the hope of the human condition. This year while we assigned Atwood's *Handmaid's Tale*, it becomes readily apparent (especially after the November 2016 election) that Orwell's *1984,* deserves the nod as required reading for our high school seniors about to embark upon the real transition to the adult world.

It becomes even more apropos given that members of this current presidential cabinet sound eerily like characters from Orwell's text (quote Kelleyanne Conway here on "alternate facts"). As an educator, I am constantly asked by my students to give them direction and guidance, especially when analyzing a character's thought or action and, in Hamlet's case, his indecision and inaction. I admonish that I cannot think for them; that they must learn to think for themselves. In shaping a young adult in today's world, the pivotal question becomes, "when should we guide and when should we let go?" Perhaps this may be a time to gently guide towards our hope in the future.

At a time such as this there are no concrete answers, but I thank God everlasting that I live in an abstract world of infinite possibilities. It is the only way for one to maintain sanity in a world that appears to be desperately seeking it. We really need to let go of still trying to analyze what "went wrong in November" and determine how we can meaningfully engage with each other (through honest and true dialogue) in order to make sure it never happens again. I think we said this after we rid ourselves of a few mad hatters in the 1940s who sounded much like the men sitting in the Oval Office right now and many of Orwell's characters on his Airstrip. It is no accident that authors such as Orwell and the poet W.H. Auden penned some of their most potent work post World War II. As Social Realism moved into its Second Phase so to speak, men such as Orwell and Auden stood at the forefront of using their pens for positive social change. There are definite lessons to be learned as Orwell's voice clearly resonates throughout this seminal text: his testament to the world is as clear as a bell: we must hold fast to the frailty of the human condition or all is truly lost to mankind. For where there is vigilance there is also hope.

I suppose the reason why I chose to teach young adults is because they are still fragile and full of hope and I refuse to teach it out of my children; yes, I have claimed them; they are not other people's children, they are mine. I take ownership of their learning and, unlike Big Brother, I refuse to program any of them to think as some would have me do in the "name of patriotism." Come to think of it, those young people didn't let anyone control their destiny either: they decided to hold fast to their humanity and seek true freedom and it was through their belief in the human condition that they too ultimately prevailed.

Ruth-Terry Walden is an African American woman born in Los Angeles, California to parents who were from East Texas (Longview) and Georgia (Augusta) respectively: part of the Great Migration that occurred during the 20th Century. While their educational opportunities were limited due to the circumstances and times that they were born in, they instilled in their children a reverence for life-long education and learning. Walden attended Wheaton College on an academic scholarship and majored in Cultural Anthropology studying under the great Ina Dinerman. After Wheaton, she attended Antioch School of Law in Washington, D.C. and obtained a J.D., moved to New York and began practicing law. As an attorney/educator and as an individual, Walden lives what she has been taught: "Every day, I impart to each and every one of my students the value of education and what it can do. That it is a means of agency and uplift, and that from the past we are able to effectively and positively change our future for the better. It is what many of our Founding Fathers (and Mothers) believed and left as a legacy to generations carrying their baton. "

They Love Big Brother

By Aaron Zwintscher

(An essay in the form of a short story)

It was an unseasonably sweltering day in April, though what even qualified as unseasonable anymore? I was just pouring my end of office hours whiskey when she appeared at the door. After a steady three-hour stream of grade grubbing and students desperate for me to all but write their essays for them, I was in no mood for more. She looked familiar but I couldn't quite put a finger on from where. It looked as if he she had been crying or running. Or both. Sweat had soaked through her thin T-shirt and the combination of the way it clung to her ample curves and the way the frigid AC in my minuscule office caused her to shudder was unseemly to say the least. If she was dropping in, hoping for some perverted father-figure-mentor relationship, she was barking up the wrong tree. This week couldn't be over soon enough.

It took me a moment to place her. Then it came to me. Last semester. Poetry. One of maybe two or three students in that "advanced" class who could actually string a sentence together, whose analysis was more than just a poorly phrased and oblivious summary. She had been the one with all the twee ironic sweaters. Huh. What was she doing here? Then out it poured.

"I'm sorry, Professor Jackson. I didn't know who else to turn to…" Well, that was a hell of a way to start off a meeting. I was getting to think that I was going to need another drink.

"Slow down, start from the beginning." I fished for her name. Something floral. Lily? Tansy? Iris? Dahlia? I sipped my whiskey. Should I offer her one? What year was she? Not worth it. Didn't need a scandal brewing so soon before tenure review.

"It's just that, well, they love him." Uh oh. Was I being brought into relationship drama? Hadn't kids these days worked that all out with the no strings and the Netflix and chill swipe righting? How could I possibly be qualified to solve this kid's dating crisis?

"Who loves whom?" Astrid. Astrid Jorgensen. Third row center. Flowers? I was way off.

"Everyone. They love Big Brother." Well, there was a curveball I hadn't expected. Had she picked up that elective on modern dystopian fiction I had seen advertised? But then why wasn't she over in Jennifer's office? If she was looking for me to help dispute a grade, I was in no mood. And what does a phrase like that even mean? Here I was calling her one of my better students and she was making facile connections to literature to explain... to explain what?

"Go on." What could she possibly mean? Love Big Brother? I mean, what with the social media and the wholesale data market, her peers had all but begged for their privacy to be invaded. Or was it that she had likely never been alive when America wasn't at war with someone?

"I just don't get it, Professor Jackson. How can people be so ignorant? How could they have voted so obviously against their own interests? How can they be so complicit in their own destruction?" Oh. That. Yeah, I suppose it was inevitable. Ignorance is Strength.

"Well, that's not a simple question. I mean, different populations and subgroups articulate their political will in different ways. And what seems like self-interest to you might be a true extension of an ideology you are not familiar with or don't accept. That said, what does an appeal to ignorance have to do with, as you put it, 'loving Big Brother?'" What a load of drivel. How many more buzzwords ya think you can spin into your nonexplanation, Nehemiah? This girl needs help and what, you think you can just name drop Foucault or Gramsci and wave a magic theory wand?

"I mean. It's just. Well, my boyfriend—ex-boyfriend, really—he voted for the rapist in chief. He said he thought it would be hilarious. And well, it's just, after your class last semester, I figured that maybe you would be able to help me to understand. How could he do that to me? How could my parents? How can half the country, be so..." I realized that she was still standing, shivering, and gestured to the chair. I walked over to raise the temp on the thermostat and used the opportunity to pour myself another whiskey. I didn't have any more classes until Monday and the stack of ungraded essays waiting on my kitchen table could wait some more. I sat behind my desk, adjusted my glasses, and sipped at the whiskey.

"I suppose it is a good thing that you and he are no longer together if your views are so divergent. As to your parents, well, I have more than my fair share of

140

disagreements with my own, as I am sure you can imagine. So how, specifically, can I help?" What is it that you are looking for, showing up to my office at the end of the day as I am trying to cut out for the weekend? What can I possibly offer you?

"You see, Dr. Steinberg, in our Dystopia in Fiction class, said that dystopias are a way of helping us understand the present. Of pointing out what's wrong in society by exaggerating it, and, like, highlighting it." So she was in Jennifer's class. And yet not in her office.

"That's certainly true. So far as it goes." But it doesn't really clarify why you ran crying into my office. I have never thought of myself as a sympathetic sort. Neither have any of my lovers or partners, for that matter. Though on that front, I would never have to worry about any of them selling me out. Not just because names were rarely exchanged. But if the police ever came looking, all my details were on Grindr, right in plain sight.

"But it's not enough. I'm reading these books and going to marches and signing petitions and I have called all my representatives in Congress — both the ones here in Florida and at home on Long Island. And ... and ... and it just feels like nothing makes a difference." Oh. Right. And in a climate like this one, in a state that inexplicably swung red, how does one keep back the inevitable despair? By looking for your keys under the streetlight.

"Well, it sounds like you are doing quite a lot. Maybe spreading yourself too thin, even. And while it might seem that nothing matters, that it nothing you do makes a difference, it's all the little things that do make a difference. Maybe not now. Maybe not in the near future. But that is certainly no reason to despair. If you don't stand up for what you believe in, who will?" I tried to keep my tone upbeat. I had my hope beaten out of me early on. But you don't grow up like I did and retain much faith in the system. Anyway, the kid looked stressed enough and didn't need my anxiety piled on top.

"Yeah. I guess. Well… um… I guess that's it. I mean, thanks for listening, Professor Jackson. I'm sure you are supposed to be on your way home now or something. It's just that sometimes everything gets a bit much, you know. And it was nice to have someone to vent to that didn't immediately say something glib about emails or corruption or child-trafficking conspiracies." How did the best of them always end up having friends that were so impossibly full of shit? Rupert's rabbit hole paranoia flashed back hard.

"That's it? Well, if you are sure. It's no problem at all, Astrid. But you might want to advise those friends of yours to get less of their news from the Internet." She rolled her eyes. We all try. But sometimes friends and friends. And it's better than drinking alone.

"Oh God, I've tried. Anyway, thanks again." She flashed a sultry smile. Had she been the one to give me my Rate My Professor chili pepper? Did she really not realize?

"Of course. Feel free to stop in anytime." And as abruptly as she had appeared, she vanished, leaving me with one hell of an unsolvable case.

* * *

After downing the last of my whiskey, I grabbed my briefcase and headed for the door. I stepped into the late afternoon heat and immediately began to perspire. Florida was sinking all right but right about now it felt like it already had. I squinted desperately, fumbling around for my sunglasses as I moved into the barest hint of a shadow cast by the Hurston English building. The weather was doing nothing to help my thinking. I needed to get home. Get to grading. Or just collapse onto the sofa and let the week drain off.

Sunglasses properly situated, I started out into the miasma. Students clogged the quad. Laughing. Sunbathing. Tossing around a Frisbee or kicking a soccer ball. The central green was full of sweet noises and an unencumbered air of delight. For all of Astrid's fears, they seemed perfectly content. Then again, what did these kids have to be concerned about? They were in college. Many of them partying several nights a week. Showing up to class and bothering to hand in homework with some regularity seemed to be the sole distractions from a life of indolent convenience. At least until the loans hit up. If only I could dream that dream again. If only every student had the privilege to be so carefree.

Thoughtcrime? Ridiculous. America didn't need to police anyone's thinking. There was room enough for everyone. There was a market for every thought and every possible aberrant behavior. So long as you paid. In fact, the more aberrant, the better. Deviation just reified the norms. Outlaw a thought and it would take hold. Forbidden fruit and all that. But let it out in the open and let people realize how inconvenient rebellion is and they will sign away all their rights without even pretending to read the EULA.

143

Burning my hands on my steering wheel pulled me from my reverie. What good was cynicism in a time like this? Astrid's earnest remarks kept nagging at me the whole drive back to my apartment. Why were we so oblivious to the con game keeping us down? Why were we so content to bargain our birthrights for a convenient meal? Why was I so willing to assume that everybody else was oblivious? Even odds they knew exactly what was coming, if not what to do about it. Maybe they were gathering their rosebuds before they settled into the undefined future of a "good job." There were any number of justifications. Ideology. Hegemony. Identity Protection. For the last few months I had been continually exhorted by my newspaper and TV to put myself in the shoes of the poor coal miner or some idealized worker laid off from a vaguely defined factory job. It still didn't add up.

I pulled into Ocean Breeze Apartments and once again drove around back to my alternate parking space. The building next to mine was being pro-cleaned after flooding again last week and my usual spot was taken by a bright red panel van promising perfect restoration and no damaged memories. Imagine. And yet the development was still in the middle of expanding, building condos across the street. Structurally sound, the manager assured me. Private and discreet. They were hoping I would buy in with a pitch that virtually guaranteed that my current place was anything but sound, private, or discreet. As if we both didn't know full well the block was virtually guaranteed to be underwater in ten years. Wasn't that why it was renting so cheap?

* * *

I shook my head at the thought, once again contenting myself that the manager hard selling me what would be a literally underwater mortgage by imagining that he wouldn't even pass one of my undergrad classes as I walked up the stairs to my unit. As if passing my class was some significant designation of worth. As if I wouldn't have passed him like the rest of the crowd so long as he showed up on time. After all, greed wasn't new. Neither were foolish investments or houses built on shifting sand. Hell, both New York and DC were built on top of swamps. Why should Florida aspire to anything different? Humans had never accepted environmental limitations before. How could they possibly think that now would be any different? So who had sold whom? We were all sleeping under the boughs of this chestnut tree.

I unlocked my door, kicked off my shoes, and dropped my briefcase on the couch. I flipped on the TV, put on the new Netflix gladiatorial competition show, and started a Seamless order. I was feeling like sushi but didn't want to go back out into the heat. Heading into the kitchen for a drink, it hit me. It really had been staring me in the face to whole time. Maybe Astrid had come by my office instead of Jennifer's in some vain attempt to enact a forbidden fantasy or because Jennifer was with another student, but we were none of us innocent.

Her ex-boyfriend, or at least a guy who had seemed like her boyfriend, had been in my class last semester too. Always had something to say even though it was almost never on topic. Loud, boisterous, confident and utterly lacking in ability. Had he been the one that argued that the importance of Yeats's "The Second Coming" was in the use of "important imagery?" He'd likely managed a B. Hadn't they all? Had anyone managed to fail that hadn't dropped out, plagiarized or neglected to turn in something to be grade inflated?

What was it my Rate My Professor page read? 'Easy grader. Just show up to class and you will pass.' Didn't I say about as much at the beginning of each class every semester? Why was Astrid so thrown by reading *1984*? Because how could she not be? The stakes of the book were so high. Everything was life and death. Love was dangerous and thought was a crime. After a childhood without risk, of course it seemed enviable. And the moral authority it offered her. I'm sure that was the best part. Knowing, truly knowing, that she was one of the woke, the enlightened, must have thrilled her for days after finishing the text. Of course, every conspiracy crank felt the same way.

I stood in my kitchen looking down at the stack of ungraded essays. It had been there untouched for over a week, even as I assured my students that I was working on them and grades would come back once they were all completed. I just couldn't bring myself to read what I knew would be at least 80% incomprehensible garbage and 20% pabulum they were certain I wanted to hear. Why did I have to always remind them that writing wasn't about the right answers? And yet the ones that bothered to take notes still assumed that I just wanted them to spit them back at me. We are all of us guilty. Maybe myself most of all.

I stared at the papers for a long time. Just stood and stared at them. They were terrible. I could tell without reading them. I knew from past semesters that they would be terrible. And I knew just the same that they would nearly all pass. Sure, I have never been told to inflate grades, but I couldn't afford the controversy either. The college had a solid reputation for academic freedom. Though every college does until it doesn't. Until the brand takes a hit. I was suddenly distressingly sober.

I couldn't keep this up. Something had to give. Something had to change. I had to change. It's always the small things. It's only the small things that matter. It is each and every one of us doing our part to live in the world we want instead of the world we accept as inevitable. And while my grade inflation was a minor thing, coming as it did after 12 years of primary and secondary "teaching to the test" that let all my students down in the first place, I was still complicit. I was still part of an education system that had seemingly no shame when graduates were capable of both writing and swallowing whole shameless propaganda. Of people who only cared about their team winning regardless of how much they or their neighbors lost. Of a system content to drive an entire generation into inescapable debt peonage. But it wasn't me, it was the system.

No. That line of bullshit was overplayed. And if education in America hadn't failed everyone since its codification, more of us would feel guilty about it.

We all loved Big Brother so long as the AC stayed cold, and the gas stayed cheap, and the sex stayed convenient. I pulled the New Amsterdam Gin from the freezer, thinned it with Publix Tonic, and struck straight in. I was feeling inspired. I was going full Jerry Maguire and was one drink away from spamming the whole college with my manifesto. I began writing about how I would give the failing students the failing grades they deserved. How I would stop stooping to the level of the worst of them and demand that they rise to the level of the best. Tenure committee be damned. Let my failing students greet me with cries of hate. I was through being complicit in a system whose best hope was a kid regurgitating slogans. With any luck, we might be able to stumble through the confusion back to a world where thinking different wasn't a branding strategy.

In all the excitement, I barely noticed the stack of essays on the kitchen table. Still untouched.

Aaron Zwintscher (@billyprophet) is a reclusive noise merchant living in Washington Heights. He has Ph.D. from the University of Central Florida in Texts & Technology and is an adjunct professor of English on Long Island. He keeps the stack of ungraded essays in his office not his kitchen. His short story was published in *The Morris-Jumel Mansion Anthology of Fantasy and Paranormal Fiction.*

Feminism in George Orwell's *1984*
By Tara Lighten Msiska

Orwell identifies lust, love, friendship, sex/orgasms and family to be what makes us human and therefore what the Party must destroy. Orwell displays a lot of liberalism here: he sees no hierarchy between lust and love (Winston's encounter with a sex worker and with Julia are favorably compared to sex with his wife. His later love for Julia is not presented as superior to her earlier lust for him).

Nor does Orwell see any preferred types of family. But in 2017 nuclear families are given the highest status and young and single parent families the lowest. Most governments try to control family life and sex, from the Nazis to Republicans and our own government's tax allowance for married but not non-married couples. The Party tried to split up couples so people would be loyal only to the government and not spouses while our present government tries to push people into marriage and keep them from divorcing so that the government's conservative moral values will be preserved against our will and against the best interests of families.

Orwell thinks that laws stop the government from oppressing us or at least limit the oppression. We tend to think that with no law there can be no crime. But Orwell thinks that without any laws anything can be a crime. Any sex that the government does not approve of is a sex crime in 1984. Similarly sex without marriage is criminalized in Dubai, cheating is criminalized in Iran and sex work is criminalized in most American states and criminalized for purchasers but not service providers in Sweden.

Orwell appears to have understood that rape is violence and not sex long before feminists brought this to public attention. Orwell presents Winston as fantasizing about raping and murdering Julia because he hates her and because she is celibate. He doesn't victim blame Julia for being slutty or wearing revealing clothes. On the contrary, it is her celibacy and political ideas which make him want to rape her. She wears the same uniform he does. This was long before the SlutWalks so it's very impressive that Orwell was so reasonable and understanding.

Julia is also a very 'slutty' character for the era in which Orwell wrote. She pursues Winston, has had many lovers since she was 16, only wants casual relationships and works fast, succeeding in sleeping with Winston almost immediately after they're alone. But Orwell never suggests she is dirty or worth less because she enjoys sex. Instead Winston seems to admire her more because she is confident enough to do what she wants instead of submitting to the sexual repression of the government. Orwell never suggests that 'sluts' deserve to be raped or can't be raped—an attitude which clearly survives to this day.

Oceania, Eastasia and Eurasia are clearly the same state under the same government. This is hinted at numerous times (Julia comments that the government itself is firing the rockets and doubts about whether the war is real). Doubts about the realness of Goldstein and the Brotherhood were proven right which seems to suggest that other doubts might be right too. The three states share the same ideology, social system and level of technology. They are three parts of a world government that continuously fakes a war to control its subjects.

The world government swaps round the fake alliances to weed out and identify citizens who can't do Doublethink. Orwell could have been hinting that ideologies or groups that seem very different from each other can oppress the citizen in the same way. Personally it is my belief that a Christian or Muslim theocracy and a radical feminist government would all oppress women and deny freedom of speech and sexual expression in similar ways. Obviously this wasn't what Orwell was writing about and I've no idea if he'd agree with me but the principle is the same.

Tara Msiska developed an interest in politics and feminism while studying Law at the University of Edinburgh, eventually writing a dissertation on EU policies and stigma against single mothers. After graduating, she started blogging and sharing her views on Twitter. This gave her the opportunity to 'meet' like-minded people and explore ideas further. The blogging led to content writing jobs and then to writing for *Mint Press News, Guerilla Policy, Cliterati* and *The Fifth Column*. Tara has just completed a Masters in International Relations and intends to progress her career in journalism.

Orwell in America — A Play
By Joe Sutton

I first had the idea of a play about Orwell in the year just before Barack Obama took office. I didn't have a very strong sense of it. Simply that Orwell's "Politics and the English Language" was such a powerful essay, and we seemed already—in those far simpler days of the Bush administration—to be heading toward an era of Doublespeak.

But then Obama did take office, and it seemed almost instantly like he faced a backlash unlike any I could recall. That backlash soon took the form of the infamous town hall meetings, and that's when the idea for my play took hold. What if Orwell had toured America? And what if in touring America he had encountered a readership unwilling to listen to what he had to say? Would his encounters have resembled the Obama era town halls?

And just what *did* he have to say? What might Orwell have told his American audience that they would have resisted? Surely it wouldn't have been about the dangers of totalitarianism, the subject of his two most famous books. After all, there's a reason he sold roughly 50 times more of his last two books

(*Animal Farm* and *1984)* than any of his earlier novels. We were caught in the Cold War. And those novels were our road map out. His audience would never have ignored or resisted him if he had spoken to them about that. So what was it?

It was the fact that he was a Socialist. That though he believed in vigilant, dedicated anti-Communism, he also believed in nationalizing Britain's railroads. And hospitals. And mine works. And that, I suspect, an American audience would not have tolerated.

And so my play is about several things, among them the relationship between an author, his work and his audience. In particular, I am interested in the politically-minded author. The author who has something to say. Who wants to *convince* people.

Well, what if he can't? What if his work is mis-read by them? What then?

Of course, my play is about something else as well. Socialism. I believed in the years just *after* the Cold War, after the danger that Orwell had worked so tirelessly to highlight, we might be open to considering how Socialism might work in America.

And who better as a tribune for the cause—than a man most Americans cannot picture, but whose name carries such powerful resonance to them. The one and only. George Orwell.

ORWELL IN AMERICA
By Joe Sutton

(AN EXCERPT OF THE FIRST 10 PAGES)

ACT ONE

THE LIGHTS COME UP ON A SELFCONSCIOUS MAN WITH AN ODD LITTLE SMILE. IN TRUTH HE'S A BIT SHY, BUT YOU CAN'T REALLY TELL IT BECAUSE HE SPEAKS SO AGGRESSIVELY.

ORWELL

My name is Eric Blair.

(AND HIS VOICE IS RATHER PLUMMYSOUNDING)

ORWELL

Now I know you've all come to see George Orwell…

(THE MAN HE ACTUALLY IS)

154

ORWELL

…but I'm afraid you'll have to make do with Eric Blair.

(HE SEEMS RATHER PLEASED WITH HIMSELF)

CARLOTTA

That's it. Come downstage.

(THIS LAST COMES FROM A WOMAN SITTING

OFF THE TO SIDE—IN SHADOWS)

ORWELL

Now of course… (ABRUPTLY, FRUSTRATED)… oh, what is it?

(HE'S FORGOTTEN HIS SPEECH)

CARLOTTA

(JUMPING IN) That's it. You're doing fine.

(BUT QUICKLY HE REMEMBERS IT)

ORWELL

This is the point where I could say that Mr. Orwell will be with you next month, Or that he's next door. (CONTINUING, EXCITEDLY) Or that the Kiwanis Club will be sponsoring a dinner on his behalf after the first of the year! But instead I'll say that I am Orwell too. (GETTING ANGRY) That is I, also, am Orwell.

Not that there are two Orwells. There is only one, and I am he!

(THIS LAST HE SAYS IRATE, FURIOUS AT HIMSELF FOR OVER-COMPLICATING. THE WOMAN INTERJECTS)

CARLOTTA

You may want to simplify that.

ORWELL

(OVERLAPPING) Which raises the question, "well then, who... is this Mr. Blair?" And the only answer is Mr. Blair was Mr. Orwell before Mr. Orwell became himself.

CARLOTTA

I -

ORWELL

(LOUDLY) May I continue? Please?!? (RESTRAINING HIMSELF) Really... I.., appreciate your... but please, do let me continue.

(HE RETURNS TO HIS AUDIENCE—HIS "IMAGINARY" AUDIENCE.)

ORWELL

That is Mr. Orwell... (ASIDE)... you may want to write down your notes in pencil ... (RESUMING THEN, TO AUDIENCE)... Mr. Orwell, the name Mr. Blair is now commonly known by, is what we call a "nom de plume". It is not his, that is my real name. My real name, the name my parents gave me, the name I took to St. Cyprian School and then on to the fields of ETON... was Blair.

CARLOTTA

Good.

ORWELL

It was Blair when I went to Burma as well. I... (THEN, SUDDENLY, BLOWING UP)... No, I'm sorry. I can't do this!

(THE LIGHTS COME UP ON A HOTEL ROOM)

CARLOTTA

Can't do what?

(AS ORWELL TURNS AROUND ON A TRULY SPECTACULAR-LOOKING WOMAN SITTING ACROSS FROM HIM. THE SCENE IS ACTUALLY TAKING PLACEJUST MOMENTS AFTER SHE'S ARRIVED. HE'S BEEN REHEARSING)

ORWELL

Practice! I'm much too distracted!

CARLOTTA

By what?

ORWELL

You!

CARLOTTA

In what sense?

ORWELL

You're too beautiful.

CARLOTTA

Oh—now—

ORWELL

Oh, don't tell me you don't know it! You know it!

CARLOTTA

Look—

ORWELL

Beside the fact—you're not what I expected.

(HE STOMPS OVER TO A SIDE TABLE —
PETULANTLY)

CARLOTTA

How so?

ORWELL

You signed your name Carlton. You said your name was Carlton!

CARLOTTA

I did, yes.

ORWELL

Why?!?

(HIS BACK IS TO HER)

CARLOTTA

(DEFENSIVELY) Because I was afraid you wouldn't see me if I signed my name Carlotta. Would you have?

ORWELL

(CERTAIN) Yes, I think so. (BEAT, LESS CERTAIN) I think I would have, yes.

CARLOTTA

Well, I couldn't be sure, and so I signed my letter Carlton. (PAUSE) Please forgive me.

(ORWELL WATCHES HER A MOMENT—THEN
SUDDENLY BLURTS OUT)

ORWELL

I need a new wife.

CARLOTTA

Pardon me?

ORWELL

My first wife is dead. I'm in need of another.

CARLOTTA

Yes, well you're also in need of a publicist.

ORWELL

Would you consider it?

CARLOTTA

Being your publicist?

ORWELL

Being my wife!

CARLOTTA

No. Mr. Orwell.

ORWELL

Mr. Blair!

CARLOTTA

Mr. Blair. No. (LONG PAUSE) But thank you for the offer.

(ORWELL UNSCREWS A WHISKEY BOTTLE. SHE WATCHES HIM. SHE IS NOW THE ONE WHO'S ANNOYED.)

CARLOTTA

Mr. Orwell.

ORWELL

(PUGNACIOUS) Blair.

CARLOTTA

Perhaps you should—

ORWELL

(SHORT) You've declined the wifely role. Have you not?

CARLOTTA

I have.

ORWELL

Very well then.

(HE NOW RETURNS WITH HIS DRINK)

ORWELL

Now then. You were saying.

CARLOTTA

(UNSURE) Up to you—I should think.

ORWELL

Where were we?

CARLOTTA

Burma.

ORWELL

Burma, yes. Burm—Actually this brings up an interesting thought. Whether I should detail the various thoughts I was having, the various "events" of my life—the travel, the fighting, Spain… Morocco… (SOMEWHAT POINTED)…my wife -whether I should detail all that…

CARLOTTA

Absolutely!

ORWELL

Or whether I should start by saying the following...

CARLOTTA

Oh, for—

ORWELL

I am a man of the Left.

(CARLOTTA'S PENCIL BREAKS)

CARLOTTA

That—

ORWELL

Whatever else you may think you have HEARD...(A BEAT)... whatever else you may KNOW...know that first and foremost. I am a man of the Left. I believe in Socialism.

CARLOTTA

You can't say that.

(THEY ARE IN THE HOTEL AGAIN)

ORWELL

Why not?

CARLOTTA

You... (FED UP) Mr. Orwell, be serious!

ORWELL

I am being serious! It's the whole point!

CARLOTTA

It is not the whole point.

ORWELL

It is!

CARLOTTA

You can't tell an American audience you're a socialist!

ORWELL

Why not?

CARLOTTA

Because of the moment we're in, that's why! Because... Mr. Orwell, could I just say two words to you? TWO WORDS! Before you go on? Animal Farm!!!!

(SHE CRIES THESE WORDS OUT!)

CARLOTTA

That's what the people want to hear. That's... People

want to hear you talk about Communism, for God's sake. The red menace. And look, I'm not saying these other topics aren't interesting. They are. But this is a book tour! And on a book tour you must talk about your book! The... here... let ... "People sleep peaceably at night"... Yes? Do you remember this?

(SHE HAS RETRIEVED A BATCH OF INDEX CARDS WHICH SHE NOW READS FROM)

CARLOTTA

"People sleep peaceably at night because ROUGH men stand ready to do VIOLENCE on their behalf." (ANOTHER CARD) "To survive it is often necessary to FIGHT. And to fight you must DIRTY yourself."

ORWELL

(SMILING, QUIETLY) You've done your research.

CARLOTTA

"War is EVIL, but it is often the LESSER... of evils." Those are ideas that people want to hear. Not... And again, I'm not saying these other ideas aren't interesting. They are. But you must give the people what they want! You—

ORWELL

(CUTTING HER OFF) I will, Miss Morrison. (BEAT) I assure you. I will.

(CARLOTTA STARES DAGGERS AT HIM)

ORWELL

But I don't think—and please, before you take issue, consider: I don't think it's best to go straight at it. I think it's best to go the way round. To... And look, I may be very wrong about this, but I think some of our audience may be very happy...to hear what I have to say about language—for instance. After all, these are literary clubs, aren't they? They're not "beer halls." Are they?

CARLOTTA

(GRUDGING) No.

ORWELL

So... let's not sell them short, shall we? Let's... (HE WINKS)... let's see what they can reach.

(AT THIS POINT THE LIGHTS SUDDENLY COME

UP ON AN AUDITORIUM, A "1940'S" AUDITORIUM...)

ORWELL

Now then, why is it IMPORTANT??

(...WHERE ORWELL, HAVING PRACTICED HIS SPEECH, IS NOW TRULY A "SHOWMAN")

ORWELL

And again, thank you so much for coming here
tonight. For being our first audience. I'm just thrilled
with this! But yes, why must we care about the
language we use; the subject we're on. I mean, good
God, what difference does it make—if we use a
German word instead of an English. Because our
thinking blurs... that's why. Because...

CARLOTTA

(IN HALF LIGHT, TO HERSELF)

Not bad.

(ORWELL GLANCES OVER AS HE SPEAKS.)

ORWELL

...when we speak in such a way, we cease to fully
EXPERIENCE what we are saying. When we adopt
these shortcuts—and this goes for pet phrases as
well—"the nub of it," "shoe on the other foot," "throw
down the gauntlet" ...when we stop thinking about
what we are saying and instead reach for the ready-
made phrase ...a reaction occurs we did not anticipate.
We begin to allow our WORDS to do our THINKING
for us. And that way...well, that way lies madness,
doesn't it? That way—and correct me if I'm wrong—
but that way the inmates are running the asylum, aren't
they? In a way? (WITH A TWINKLE) As it were?

(AGAIN HE GLANCES OVER AT CARLOTTA,

HIS EYEBROWS RAISED)

ORWELL

Do you see? A joke.

CARLOTTA

(AMUSED) I… yes.

ORWELL

You're not laughing.

CARLOTTA

I'm… inside I am.

(CONTINUING, WITHOUT PAUSE)

ORWELL

In any case, Blair, Orwell, who is he?

Joe Sutton has had a prestigious career as a playwright and has taught playwriting at such leading professional institutions as New Dramatists in New York City and the HB Studios, also in New York. His work has been produced by such theaters as London's Old Vic, Seattle Rep, New York Theatre Workshop, BAM, Arena Stage, Long Wharf, the Old Globe, as well as other theaters around the country and abroad. In addition to receiving fellowships from the National Endowment for the Arts and the New York Foundation for the Arts, Professor

Sutton's work has been nominated for the Pulitzer Prize and for the "Best Play" by the American Theatre Critics Association. He has also won the FDG/CBS Playwriting Award and the Beverly Hills Theater Guild Playwriting Award. His work has been published by Oberon Books, TCG, Dramatists Play Service, and Broadway Play Publishing. This year marks Professor Sutton's seventeenth year of teaching playwriting at Dartmouth. The summer of 2006, his play GUNS&AMMO premiered on campus. Professor Sutton is an alumnus of Dartmouth.

Coming to a Theater Near You, Again

By Adam Birnbaum and Dylan Skolnick

Who and what is the United State of Cinema?

The United State of Cinema is an informal and ever-growing collective of venues located throughout the United States (along with a few in Canada and abroad) that wish to provide an opportunity for communities around the country to show their unity and have their voices heard through the exhibition and contextualization of select films that carry some form of social, political or cultural currency.

How did the idea for this national protest screening of *1984* come about? Has something like this even been done before?

Dylan and I frequently commiserate about a wide range of subjects, from our opinions and predictions about current movie releases, new programming ideas and initiatives, to topics unrelated to our business endeavors, such as our deeply shared anxiety about the dire state of affairs in the United States. We concurred with one another that we each felt a sense of social responsibility to be more active in some tangible capacity, and arrived at the conclusion that one productive means could be via the utilization and mobilization of independent cinemas throughout the country to collectively exhibit films that made a statement. Dylan ultimately proposed to me the idea of kicking things off by screening "1984" for all apparent topical reasons and from there we were off to the races in organizing this event.

How did you implement this showing at so many theaters throughout the country?

This process unfolded entirely in a truly grassroots, all-volunteer, all hands on deck fashion, without a single dollar spent. It began with Dylan and myself drafting a letter that spelled out our objectives and the steps needed to be taken to participate. We subsequently emailed the letter out to cinemas that we either directly represent as film buyers, or with which we have existing relationships, including venues that participate in the Art House Convergence. We relied on the help of friends to create a very simple website, Facebook page and Twitter account, and enlisted the support of a publicist, Alex Klenert at Prodigy Public Relations, who generously donated his time to garner significant national press for the cause. From there we piggybacked off of the coverage and proliferating word of mouth among like-minded venues to enroll close to 200 participating theaters.

What are you hoping to achieve with this national protest screening?

While this effort is primarily about raising awareness about the existence and actions of a totalitarian regime in the United States, and the extent to which there are concerned citizens who unequivocally object to fascism, it is also about increasing collaborative programming efforts among independent cinemas in a fashion that is relevant to said current socio-political circumstances, so as to utilize these venues as community-building conduits that foster a collective consciousness. This nation is presently so fractured, the government so completely fraudulent, its new "leadership" simultaneously a farce and a fear-inducing menace with a mob-like mentality, that many people feel a great sense of hopelessness and alienation. We hope that in some small way this screening can offer a foundation for individuals to feel a call to action on a localized, community level, and to know that it is not only OK but quite necessary in the present environment to more actively express objections. Or that it will simply stimulate other arts organizations, activist groups, students, educators, religious, political and other community leaders to take a more active role in protesting what is happening here.

Are there plans for additional protest screenings?

We have discussed and toyed with the idea of additional screenings with different content, and do indeed hope that if this one is well supported and effective that it will be the start of something ongoing. In fact, there is already a movement underway by fellow like-minded programmers called The Seventh Art Stand, in which venues will be showcasing films from the countries affected by the attempts on the part of the government to enact a Muslim travel ban. Not only do we think that's great, we hope that more programmers will feel galvanized to take the requisite steps to organize activist screenings.

Adam Birnbaum is the founder and president of the Nova Theatre Circuit, a film buying, booking and consulting firm started in 2005, which presently represents nearly 40 independently owned and operated movie theatres throughout the Northeast, Mid-Atlantic, Southeast, and Pacific Northwest regions of the United States. Many of the venues he handles are historic downtown theatres and/or nonprofit community cinemas, which have collectively lent themselves to his established niche in the art house/specialized sector of the film exhibition industry.

Adam is also the Director of Film Programming for the Avon Theatre Film Center in Stamford, CT, a landmark 1939 art deco movie house. Working in that capacity since 2003, he has contributed to the team effort from the organization's inception to reopen and resurrect the formerly shuttered theatre, transforming it into a regionally recognized cinema arts institution.

Dylan Skolnick is Co-Director at the Cinema Arts Centre, Long Island's leading venue for alternative film. He maintains the Centre's 40-plus year focus on using film to expand the awareness and understanding of Long Islanders to the vital local and global issues facing our society. The Cinema Arts Centre Co-Directors have received honors for community impact from many organizations, including the Long Island Progressive Coalition, PAX Christi, Planned Parenthood, NYCLU, and the NOW Alliance PAC of Long Island.

Mr. Skolnick is a Consultant and Film Buyer for a number of Cinemas across the USA, including the Circle Cinema in Tulsa, Oklahoma, the Hollywood Theater in Pittsburgh, Pennsylvania, the Art Mission and Theater in Binghamton, New York, the Old Greenbelt Theatre in Greenbelt, Maryland, and the Lyric Theatre in Stuart, Florida.

About the Editor

Lori Perkins is a published author, book editor and literary agent with three decades experience in publishing newspapers and books, She was the owner and publisher of the *Upton Weekly News* in Manhattan's Washington Heights and Inwood in the 80's, as well as an adjunct professor of journalism at NYU. She has written or edited 30 books, 25 of which have been erotic romance anthologies. She was the editor of the very first zombie romance anthology, *Hungry for Your Love*, and the editor of the nonfiction collection of essays *50 Writers on 50 Shades of Grey*. She is the founder of both the L. Perkins Agency, an established New York literary agency with numerous books on the *New York Times* bestseller list, as well as the Publisher of Riverdale Avenue Books, an award-winning hybrid publisher. She is currently working on a series of naughty historicals with *USA Today* bestselling author Jamie Schmidt under the nom de plume Lorna James. You can follow her on Twitter at LoriPerkinsRAB.

Other Riverdale Avenue Books Anthologies You Might Like

Bi Any Other Name: Bisexual People Speak Out
Edited by Lani Ka'ahumanu and Loraine Hutchins

Finding Masculinity: Female to Male Transition in Adulthood
Edited by Alexander Walker and Emmett J.P. Lundberg

Outside the XY: Queer Black and Brown Masculinity
Edited by Bklyn Boihood

Leaving the Rest
Gay Men on Alcoholism, Addiction and Recovery
Edited by Dr. Gerald Perlman

We Love New York:
A Romance Anthology to Raise Funds for Hurricane Sandy Relief
Edited by Trinity Blacio and Lori Perkins

The Circlet Treasury of Erotic Steampunk
Edited by Cecilia Tan

The Circlet Treasury of Lesbian Erotic Science Fiction and Fantasy
Edited by Cecilia Tan

The Circlet Treasury of Erotic Alice in Wonderland
Edited by J. Blackmore

Printed in Great Britain
by Amazon